.

WAKING UP *to the* DARK

WAKING UP
to the DARK

Ancient Wisdom for a Sleepless Age

CLARK STRAND

Illustrations by Will Lytle

SPIEGEL & GRAU / NEW YORK

Published in the United States by Spiegel & Grau,
an imprint of Random House, a division of Random House LLC,
a Penguin Random House Company, New York.

SPIEGEL & GRAU and the HOUSE colophon
are registered trademarks of Random House LLC.

ISBN 978-0-8129-9772-9

eBook ISBN 978-0-8129-9773-6

Printed in the United States of America on acid-free paper

www.spiegelandgrau.com

1 2 3 4 5 6 7 8 9

First Edition

Book design by Susan Turner

For Sophie,
who walks with me in the dark . . .

And Mary answered and said,
"What is hidden from you, I will proclaim."

—THE GOSPEL OF MARY 5:7

CONTENTS

WHEN THE PEOPLE OF MY SMALL MOUNTAIN TOWN GOT THEIR first dose of electrical lighting in late 1924, "they were appalled by the brightness and crudity of the resulting illumination," wrote local historian Alf Evers. As Christmas approached, a protest was staged on the village green denouncing the evils of modern light.

"Old people swore that reading or living by so fierce a light was impossible." Besides which, it was a matter of pride: "Every flaw in their household furnishings was shown up." That much light invited comparisons. It threw everything in sharp relief. It was an advertisement for the new, the rich, and the beautiful — a verdict against the old, the ordinary, and the poor.

A few days later the naysayers got their way. The power failed, and Christmas on the village green was celebrated with nothing but candlelight to pierce the solstice, the darkest time of the year. I've searched the annals of the town to see if there were any further protests before it went fully electric a year or so later, but I haven't found any. Here as elsewhere in early twentieth-century America, the reluctance to embrace brighter lights was a brief and halfhearted affair.

People sensed there was something wrong with the new technology. They just couldn't say what it was. All but the most cantankerous felt foolish to oppose a product as clean and cheap as electrical light. It was so cheerful and convenient and downright wholesome that any argument against it seemed wrongheaded, maybe even evil. After all, what good Christian would argue in favor of the dark?

There was no stopping the century of progress for which Edison's invention was literally the guiding light. Who could have known it was the worst thing that could happen to the planet? We don't know the value of darkness until we have destroyed it. We don't know what a soul is worth until it is gone.

Part I

HOUR *of the* WOLF

I AM NOT AFRAID OF THE DARK.

My wife insists that this is the reason people listen when I speak on spiritual matters. I spent years studying Zen Buddhism. After that, I immersed myself in spiritual practices from all over the world. But none of that made me wiser or more enlightened than anyone else. It isn't the reason people listen.

From childhood on I have woken up in the middle of the night and sought out the darkness. Not only am I not afraid of it, I love it more than anything. That's what people are drawn to without knowing it. It's important to them for reasons they find difficult to explain. It's as if I've reminded them of something they once knew, but can now no longer recall.

As a young child in Alabama, I began slipping out into the night whenever I could. We lived in a small town in a house only one block from the golf course. I loved the big heady silence of the starry fairways and the pockets of darkness in the trees between the links that almost seemed absolute.

Once, when I was caught coming home, my mother demanded to know what I had been doing, and I pretended I had been sleepwalking. I wasn't a noticeably eccentric child, but I knew there was something strange about my nighttime wanderings. My mother believed the lie, or probably she just chose to believe. After all, I was wearing shoes. But it was just as well. What drove me on these midnight rambles? I would have been at a loss to explain, even if she had asked.

By the time I was a teenager, I was often walking five miles or more in the middle of the night. I strolled through backyards and graveyards, found my way through fences and fields. I felt profoundly at home in the dark. We moved so often when I was a child that it was hard for me to find the kind of comfortable footing with friends and teachers that most children take for granted. So my inner home, my dream home, became the darkness itself.

I went to a college situated atop a large plateau and surrounded by thousands of acres of wilderness. I hiked at night, discovering caves and cliffs. I climbed water towers and visited abandoned barns. I felt protected, not just by the bounds of the university, but by nature itself. Out in the fields under the stars alone, I had no one to please but myself.

I never carried a flashlight. The nights were rarely so dark, even in the country, that you couldn't feel your way along a path or road. I once hiked up a mountain in complete darkness on a summer night with a thick canopy of leaves blocking out the sky. There was no moon. I listened to the sounds my feet made on the pebbles of the path. If I stepped on leaves, I corrected myself and found the trail again. After two hours I arrived at the summit and finally saw the stars.

It was a wonder my health didn't suffer from lack of sleep, but it never did. Even then I was on the verge of knowing something about darkness and the human body, and about consciousness and our relationship to the divine and how they all depended on each other. But I had no framework then for that understanding. It was entirely experiential. Even later, in the midst of my Zen training, I would not connect my night-time rambles through the monastery graveyard with the concerted training I was undergoing in the meditation hall. It never occurred to me that out in the inky blackness of the mountains I was on the trail of a deeper, more ancient practice all but forgotten to the world.

. . .

MANY OF US WAKE UP IN THE MIDDLE OF THE NIGHT AND CAN'T get back to sleep.

We worry about our money and our health. About our kids and our marriages. About how little sleep we are getting and how tired we will be the following day. We often turn on the lights to get through those sleepless hours. Or we surf the Internet or watch TV. My father read scores of tedious, half-forgotten Victorian novels to span the midnight hours. Sometimes we take a pill our doctor has prescribed to manage insomnia, rather than risk waking up in the dark.

In the darkness there are no distractions from the worries of ordinary life. In the light we can organize them, or compartmentalize them, or hide them where we won't see them — as if shoving them into the dark. But *inside* of the dark? Inside the dark we are unprotected, and our troubles always come close. So close we can hear them breathing. So close we sometimes feel paralyzed with fear, unable to flee or even move. So close they could open their mouths and swallow us . . . or settle down for a long leisurely *gnaw.*

No wonder we dread waking up in the dark. We'd rather stay up late and fall exhausted into a dreamless sleep that leaves us hollowed out in the morning, remembering nothing — feeling not so much like we've slept as been anesthetized. Which, if we've taken sleep medication on top of everything else, we have been.

In popular idiom, that waking period between dark and daybreak is called the "Hour of the Wolf," an image evoking the eerie, predatory fatalism that tends to come calling in the small hours of the night. It is believed to be the hour when most people die and when the nightmares we wake from are likeliest to seem real. It is the hour when the sleepless are haunted by secret fears — when the ghosts and demons they scarecely believe in by daylight suddenly come to life. Supposedly, it is also the hour when most babies are born.

A little research reveals that the claims for births and deaths are exaggerated. Nevertheless, for those who lie awake in the hours after midnight, the mythology surrounding the Hour of the Wolf is entirely believable. Birth, death, psychic trauma — those all seem right on point.

There is something dire about the hour between dark and dawn. It is the time when human beings are at their most vulnerable—when Special Forces soldiers are taught to attack, and when the secret police under Hitler and Stalin knew they were least likely to meet with resistance when they came to take "undesirables" away. It is the hour of shifting tides, when the darkness swells and surges, when its waters rise above our heads.

. . .

On my nighttime rambles, I have never run into trouble, even when I was inexperienced and young. As a teenager I walked the hills north of Atlanta in the small hours of the night. Admittedly, it was a gentler city then. Still, no one ever bothered me.

I certainly don't like the contrived darkness of cellars and closets and alleyways. Outdoors, at night, however, I have never felt afraid.

Am I made differently from most people? Surely there are others who feel this way about the night, others who love its monochrome wonders, its velvety silences and distant muffled sounds. Yet in my rural town I almost never run into anyone on my nightly walks—except for one eccentric, a man everyone calls Jogger John.

Once or twice a year our paths cross, always in summer. John rides his bike on moonless nights, singing joyously to himself as he goes. On such occasions, he seems as surprised to see me as I am him. But neither of us is frightened. He zips by in what appears to be utter blackness. His eyes must be even better than mine. Or maybe he is only joyously reckless on those nights when he dares a downhill ride in the dark.

I've asked myself what we have in common, John and I. There isn't much on the surface. But there is one thing, I suppose. When the wolf arrives, he doesn't find us fretting in our beds. We're up before him and out in the darkness, where the night and the wolf are one.

. . .

MOST PEOPLE ASSUME THAT WAKING UP IN THE MIDDLE OF THE night is unnatural. Even our doctors assume as much. When we were young parents, my wife and I initially believed what the baby books told us about teaching our daughter to sleep through the night. Eventually, however, her distress was too much for us and we brought her into our bed. There she would happily nurse from my wife, who now didn't have to get out of bed or even fully awaken. Often when I woke in the middle of the night, I would find her sitting up between us, serene and smiling, happily gazing at the moon.

During the mid-1990s, about the same time our daughter was born, a lead researcher at the National Institute of Mental Health conducted an experiment he later called an exercise in "archaeology, or human paleobiology." Dr. Thomas Wehr wanted to find out if modern humans still carried within them the rhythms for a prehistoric mode of sleep.

The logic of Wehr's study was simple: Aided by the stimulating effects of all kinds of artificial lighting (everything from laptop screens to the bright lights of big cities), modern humans had compressed their sleep nights, like their workdays, into convenient eight-hour blocks. And yet, given that light-assisted wakefulness was a relatively new invention, wasn't it possible that human beings still carried in their DNA the remnants of a more primordial pattern of sleep?

Did prehistoric humans sleep more? Did they sleep differently—or perhaps better? These were the questions Wehr wanted to answer.

The results were staggering. For one month, beginning at dusk and ending at dawn, Wehr's subjects were removed from every possible form of artificial lighting—even the gentle glow of a luminescent clock. During the first three weeks, they slept as usual, only for about an hour longer. (After all, he reasoned, like most Americans, they were probably sleep deprived.) But at week four a dramatic change occurred. The participants slept the same number of hours as before, but now their sleep was divided in two. They began each night with approximately four hours of deep sleep, woke for two hours of what Wehr termed "quiet rest," and then slept for another four.

During the gap between their first and second sleep, Wehr's subjects were neither awake nor fully asleep. Rather, they experienced a condition they had never known before—a state of consciousness all its own. Later Wehr would compare it to what advanced practitioners experience at the deepest levels of meditation. But there weren't any such practitioners in his study. They were simply ordinary people who, removed for one month from artificial lighting, found their nights broken in half—or maybe broken *open*. Because there was something hidden inside.

While trying to account for the peace and serenity that his subjects reported feeling during their hours of "quiet rest," Wehr discovered that the hormone *prolactin* reached elevated levels in their bodies shortly after dusk, remaining at twice its normal waking level throughout the full length of the night. Even during the hours of quiet rest, their prolactin levels remained steady. Normally, if you wake in the night, those levels will go down—even if you don't turn on the lights. But if you turn the lights off at dusk and *keep* them off, giving your body the full spectrum of the night to work from, that richer, deeper darkness will fashion an experience so different from the Hour of the Wolf you might as well call it the Hour of God.

Prolactin is the hormone that keeps birds still while they are sitting on their eggs and mammals quietly at rest while they are sleeping. Its levels also rise in nursing mothers when their milk lets down, keeping them calm and attentive to their babies' needs. In recent years, it has been called the "attachment hormone" because of its role in early bonding between mothers and infants. Prolactin creates a feeling of security, quietness, and peace. And it is intimately, and biologically, tied to the dark. Enter the darkness, and *stay* there—without checking your cell phone or turning on the lights—and the darkness, like a mother or a lover, will take you in her embrace.

"I sleep, but my heart is awake," says the Song of Songs, a sacred love poem written at a time when that quiet nightly waking must still have been a common occurrence. It isn't a teaching or a spiritual metaphor. It describes an actual state of mind. It's the state sometimes experienced by lovers after their lovemaking, awake and still touching, in the stillness and silence of the night. Or the state of mind of a child rising, for reasons he cannot comprehend and his culture has forgotten, to walk alone on a golf course in the middle of the night.

Two thousand years ago the sage who wrote the shortest and most mysterious of Hindu texts, the Mandukya Upanishad, described this state of consciousness as the last of four such states. The first was *waking*, the second was *dreaming*, the third was a *dreamless sleep*. To the last he gave no name except *Turiya*, "the Fourth"—a state beyond all of the others, but which somehow also contained them. It was a transcendent state—neither conscious nor unconscious, known or unknown. It was indestructible, inconceivable, indescribable, but still filled to brimming with *Itself*. It was *Atman*, the soul, the point of human life. But it had to be experienced. It could not be captured in words.

And yet, once upon a time everyone *did* experience that fourth state of consciousness, because they woke to it in the middle of the night.

"This is a state not terribly familiar to modern sleepers," Wehr lamented when the study was done and he had begun to wrap his mind around the enormity of a discovery that turned modern consciousness on its head. "Perhaps what those who meditate today are seeking is a state that our ancestors would have considered their birthright, a nightly occurrence." He might have added that this was probably what all religions were seeking to preserve—a state of well-being that is probably the closest we've ever come as a species to the experience of oneness with the divine, a nightly meditation retreat for all *Homo sapiens* on Earth.

Recently, as a result of Wehr's study and others like it, some sleep specialists have reported that the best treatment for the Hour of the Wolf is to tell patients that nightly waking is natural and, consequently, that they shouldn't struggle against it. A doctor told me that once he explained this to them, many of his patients simply went to bed earlier each night and never asked him for sleep medications again. Had he conducted a follow-up study of those patients, I'm sure he'd have discovered that they were more spiritually content as well.

*   *   *

TODAY, WHEN OUR WORLD IS SO HIGHLY ILLUMINATED, WE stand at a distinct disadvantage in seeking to understand the "twilit" teachings of bygone peoples for whom the rhythms of darkness and light were intertwined with what Homer referred to as the "first" and "second" sleep of the night. Much of what we call myth or spiritual wisdom was born out of that ancient liminal space.

The oldest word for meditation in the Western canon is the Hebrew word *suwach*, a word that appears only once in the Bible: "And Isaac went out to *meditate* in the field at the eventide" (Genesis 24:63). Because the word is so old and so rare, its precise meaning is now uncertain—as if it were the artifact of an older practice that, even then, was already disappearing from the world. It may, for instance, have meant not only to meditate, but to pray, chat, meander, mutter, walk, or even complain. Mostly likely, it referred to a flexible state of mind that could be one thing one moment and another the next. It doesn't resemble anything we would call meditation today. But then, in the light-saturated hours that now pass for waking consciousness, perhaps we have forgotten what that is.

In every religion there is a long-established tradition, usually initiated by its founder, that involves waking in the middle of the night for some kind of spiritual practice—for meditation, for chanting, or for prayer. The reports of various contemplatives I have talked to over the years—monks and nuns, priests and rabbis, imams and lamas—reveal a single pattern at work. After about four hours of sleep, they would awaken to perform their devotions, during which time their minds occupied a space that wasn't quite waking, and wasn't really dreaming either, but seemed to have qualities of both. It was a visionary state, a time of deep tranquillity during which they felt especially forgiven, blessed, or loved.

Muslims believe God draws physically closer to listen to prayers in the middle of the night. In Islam the Hour of God is called *Tahajjud*, the "Night Prayer." Considered optional for pious Muslims, it was initiated by Muhammad, who taught that the form of devotion most loved by Allah was "the prayer of David, who would sleep half the night, then get up and pray for a third of the night, then sleep for a sixth of the night."

In Judaism this time is called *Tikkun Chatzot*, the "Midnight Repair." A private service to mourn the loss of the temple at Jerusalem, it is now observed only among cabalists (albeit rarely) and in certain Hasidic sects. Fittingly, the noun *chatzot* comes from a Hebrew root meaning "to cut in two." Thus *Tikkun Chatzot* refers to a spiritual practice that divides the first and second sleeps of the night. Says one rabbinical authority, "The time for Chatzot starts six hours after nightfall, both in the summer and in the winter, and continues for two hours." This corresponds exactly with what Thomas Wehr discovered in his studies on sleep, given that his subjects lay quietly for two hours beginning at dusk, after which they slept for four hours before waking to the Hour of God.

Among Christians the "Night Office" is now observed only by the most strictly "enclosed" Catholic monks. A Carthusian novice master told me that his order had kept the tradition alive from the time of its founding over nine hundred years ago. Brother Mary Joseph Kim had no idea that the practice was much older than that. Nevertheless, he, too, corroborated Wehr's findings.

> For me personally it was the experience of the Night Office that attracted me to the Charterhouse. For most of us here, this time of prayer is the most important. There is a freshness of spirit, an emptiness of mind, a depth of heart, which we don't have during the day. The structure of the Night Office: singing the Psalms, listening to the readings, praying in silence, allows one to remain a long time recollected without any notable effort and to continue the "prayer of the heart."

He explained that the Night Office always began after midnight and lasted for about two hours. This, he assured me, was incomparably the best time for being with God.

In Hinduism the Hour of God is found in scriptures like the Mandukya Upanishad, and in practices like *yoga nidra* (or "yogic sleep"). Buddhism, too, is replete with practices reminiscent of the dark gospel. The high priest at Taiseki-ji Temple in Japan has chanted the *Ushitora Gongyo* service continuously every night for the past eight hundred years. *Ushi* refers to the hour of the ox, *tora* to that of the tiger. Thus, the service is performed between 2 and 4 a.m.

Not surprisingly, the Buddha's enlightenment is said to have occurred during that time. According to legend, that was the hour when Shakyamuni turned the tables on the tempter Mara, transforming the Hour of the Wolf into the Hour of God.

The list could go on indefinitely. In fact, we might compile a book that consisted of nothing *but* that list. But the effort would be pointless. Such practices are the proverbial "higher ground" to which the Hour of God has retreated against the rising tide of electrical light. Does it really matter if someone somewhere preserves it, if in the rest of the world it is gone? The Hour of God is analogous to what the late MIT professor Stephen M. Meyer called a "ghost species"—a plant or animal that endures as a persistent ecological illusion, although its numbers have fallen to the point where it is functionally extinct. It won't make a comeback, although you may still run across one every now and then.

Fortunately for us, the metaphor of species extinction applies only to institutional manifestations of the Hour of God. The good news is that religiously sponsored observances might *all* die out—religion itself might die out—and the darkness would remain. Reclaiming it is as simple as turning out the lights.

. . .

I WOULD NOT PRESUME TO TELL ANYONE HOW BEST TO PRAY AT night. There is a kind of divine therapy that works naturally, even spontaneously, between the first and second sleeps of the night. But to benefit from that therapy, we have to awaken to darkness. We have to witness it for ourselves, and receive *its* witness, because it has many things to tell us. The darkness has a gospel to relate.

The point of life has little to do with the getting and spending that occupies the greater portion of our days. If we want to know the value of life—the *real* value, not the monetary or social value—we have to wake up in the middle of the night and see what is happening in the dark.

Are there dreams and visions? Are there symbols and signs? Is the night palpable with hopes and longings, pregnant with intimations and desires? Can we hear the peepers in the woods? The quiet of the snowfall? The rise and fall of someone's breath? Or is our impulse to turn on the lights, watch television, or medicate ourselves back into unconsciousness?

I, too, sometimes wake to the Hour of the Wolf instead of the Hour of God, though this seldom occurs when I have let the darkness have its way. It usually happens when I am over-worked or overtired. Then I worry about the usual things. About paying my children's tuition for college, about my health, about the car that needs fixing, or the assignment I have due at the end of the week and am having trouble writing.

But the darkness has taught me that most of these worries are not truly my own. They have been passed along to me from the daylit world as if they were precious things. Society creates them, I suppose. But I take them on, believing them to be im-portant, and carry them into the night. "Take no thought for the morrow," said Jesus in the Sermon on the Mount, "for the morrow shall take thought for the things of itself. Sufficient unto the day is the evil thereof." It was a caution against letting the worries of the day seep into the peace of night.

The daylight realm teaches us that we are here to fulfill all kinds of human ambitions. To grow wealthy, or influential, or powerful. Or even to become wise, albeit in a worldly kind of way. We are to make discoveries, make progress, prove our use-fulness, and improve the overall quality of human life. But maybe all we are supposed to do is keep the lights off in the middle of the night. In fact, simple as it is, I am now quite cer-tain that is so.

If someone asked me why I rise to walk at night, I couldn't answer except to say that I do it for its own sake, for the sake of rising and walking and praying in the dark. That time of con-templation and communion is its own reward. It creates its own culture in the soul. But in the past hundred years, that inner culture—that *soul* space—has become increasingly well lit.

Much of the world now lives in areas too bright to see the

Milky Way. It has become harder and harder to find natural darkness. Inside our homes, outside on our streets, inside our very heads, the lights are always on. In the conquest of human consciousness, the incandescent bulb has been the conquistador convinced of his sacred duty to explore and reform the night, converting the darkness to light.

· · ·

AND THE LIGHTS ARE EVERYWHERE. THEY ARE SO PERVASIVE IN modern life we've stopped seeing them. In turning them off, it's hard to know where to begin.

There are house lights and garage lights, fluorescent lights and halogen lights. There are streetlights and stoplights, headlights, taillights, dashboard lights, and billboard lights. There are night-lights to stand sentinel against the dark of our rooms and hallways, and reading lights for feeding our addiction to words and images and information, even in the middle of the night. There are warning lights and safety lights, and the lights of our cell phones and televisions and computer screens. No wonder our larger towns and cities are so bright you can see them from space. Nor does that urban and suburban light stay put. It seeps into the nearby plains and hills and mountains, casting shadows from trees and telephone poles. It throws off the rhythms of insects and animals and confuses the migrations of birds.

But it's not just the light *sources* that are everywhere—it's the light surfaces, too.

Everything in our environment is made to throw off light. We aren't satisfied just to *have* good light—we've remade our whole reality in the *image* of light. It bounces off every floor and countertop, off glossy finishes and polishes, off the stainless steel fixtures and appliances that define every aspect of contemporary life—even off the buildings of our urban skyline. By night those buildings light up like beacons, even after everyone has gone home. By daylight their windows reflect the sun and sky. We think they serve the interests of culture or commerce, but really they are temples to light.

It's hard for most of us to remember when we last experienced true darkness—darkness without a clock dial, or the sleep indicator on a computer that, in reality, "sleeps" about as well as we do. We can't shut our eyes to the light when our consciousness is so saturated with it. Like our computers, we're still plugged in and blinking at intervals throughout the night. We've taken in so much light during our artificially lengthened days, and from every angle and direction, that it's often impossible to let go of it, even at 1 or 2 a.m. How many of us lie down to sleep only to find images from the nightly news or TV advertisements playing like a movie inside our brains?

But waking in the darkness clears the slate.

Somehow all the excess illumination and information of the day gets lost after only four hours of real sleep in total darkness. It'll all come back with daybreak, but in the middle of the night there can be a reprieve. The light doesn't own me when I wake to utter blackness. It cannot enter my mind.

Sadly, though, even in the country I cannot take the darkness for granted. There hasn't been a robbery on my road for so long that the locals rarely bother to lock their doors. But there are weekenders from the city, second-home owners who are convinced that their property must be protected by motion-activated lights. In some of the darkest, most silent passages of my nightly pilgrimage, a porch light will flash on because I've tripped an invisible beam. I've learned where they are, so I am able to walk around them for the most part, but sometimes I forget. Or, lost in prayer, I don't notice until they come on. And then, of course, there are the houses with exterior lights that shine perpetually.

The houses that trouble me most are the ones with a lamp on all night and people living inside. I don't look at those lamps and think what a waste of electricity or money they are. It's another waste I see. For every watt that shines in the darkness, I see restless sleepers drifting further and further from their souls. It's why we can't experience love, or a feeling of safety or security during the day. It's why we worry and can't enjoy sex. For sex belongs to the darkness, not the light. It was born there, and lives there, as surely as the moon belongs to the night.

· · ·

BEFORE THE INVENTION OF GAS AND INCANDESCENT LIGHTING, most people went to bed within an hour or two of dusk. Candles were expensive, oil more so. There was light if you needed it, but it wasn't enough to turn back the tide of the night. Once the sun went down, the darkness began to roll in from all directions until it completely swallowed the land. There was no resisting it. It was a universal fact of life.

People instinctively headed home as that time approached. You wanted to be settled in before night. By daylight you could travel as needed, journeying here and there to attend to the business of life. By darkness only the most urgent matters led to venturing forth—to fetch the doctor when someone was ill, for instance, or the midwife when a baby was being born. People strolled sometimes by moonlight, and they might wander by starlight into a nearby field, to pray or check on the animals . . . or sometimes both. But the darkness kept them on a short tether. The other end was tied to the bedroom, which at nighttime became the center of their world.

The night life was very different from what it is today. No one was coming home after midnight. No one was in the next room on the computer or watching TV. Everyone was in bed, sometimes for a dozen hours at a time, depending on the season. It was a time for storytelling and listening, musing and imagining, sleeping and dreaming, and—in the middle of it, after waking from the first sleep—a time for making love. Maybe it isn't true that most babies were born during that time, but it was almost certainly when most of them were being made.

What was it about the darkness that lent itself to love? Privacy was surely a part of it. And then, in an era that included much less leisure, most people were tired at the end of the day. They woke rested after the first sleep, lying right next to one another in the dark . . . quiet and awake.

But it wasn't only that.

The Hour of God was perfect for lovemaking. For prayer

isn't the only thing sacred in the dark. Absent the troubles of the day, people could more easily relax and let go—of fears and worries, of false hopes and expectations . . . of everything. The darkness also helped them to accept and honor one another. Light invited comparisons and judgments. It exposed what appeared to be flaws but really weren't—the belly that sagged after the birth of children, the wrinkles from a lifetime of working in the sun. The darkness not only forgave these, it celebrated them. You were as old as you looked by daylight, as young as you felt by night.

Strangely, sex wasn't something they talked a lot about by daylight, even though sex was probably a lot more intimate in those days. What passed between lovers in the dark hours was invisible, indescribable, and unseen. Perhaps that was the reason they didn't speak much about it. They couldn't describe it. Or they didn't want to—not because they were modest, but because they didn't want to break the spell.

Most people today would probably claim that they are sexually liberated compared with people living only a century or two ago. For one thing, birth control has allowed women a sexual freedom they could never have experienced otherwise. For another, in most educated circles homosexuality is no longer regarded as a sin. But something has been lost when couples, straight or gay, no longer wake to embrace each other in the silence and privacy of the dark.

Outwardly liberated, many of us are so exhausted and sleep deprived we can rarely wake ourselves for sex in the middle of the night. Even more tragically, when we do, the lights in our heads are always on. Our thousand-watt culture has left so few shadows, particularly when it comes to sex, that there is now no place left in the world to experience our lovemaking but in the full light of consciousness. It's as if the dimmer switch we were born with has been broken—by advertisements, by movie and television images, by sexting and sex tapes and even sex therapy—so that now it has only two settings: On and Off. With the switch off, we're unconscious. With it on, we're at the mercy of light. The light stimulates us, that much is certainly true, but in so doing it shifts our experience of the sensual from the body into the mind.

How are we who spend so much time in the light to recover that inner dimness that dissolves the borders between bodies and that is the universal precondition for physical and spiritual rapture of any kind?

In the Song of Songs, the only book of the Bible that celebrates both darkness and erotic love, two lovers rendezvous in closed rooms and shadowy bowers, making their way by taste and touch and smell until they find each other's bodies in the dark. The Song of Songs was the most widely commented-upon book of scripture during the Middle Ages—more popular even than the gospels—and the reason was simple. It wasn't read as an erotic love poem that somehow made its way into the Bible. It was a manual for mystical union—a guide for the care of the human soul.

Sex belongs to nature and to darkness. It does not belong to a world supersaturated with images, with information, and with light. The more we look at it, the more forced and unnatural it becomes. It belongs to the world of touch, to skin and lips and fingertips. It does not belong to sight. It's the reason why most of us instinctively close our eyes to kiss. And the reason why lovers—*true* lovers—are happiest with no one watching, not even themselves, alone and quiet in the dark.

. . .

I HAVE NOT DESCRIBED HOW DARKNESS FEELS AGAINST THE skin. Everyone has felt it, but in an age when consciousness itself is no longer consciousness, but only a by-product of wattage, most people have forgotten the feeling of the dark.

The darkness fits the body so well that we might as well be entering the water when we wear it. It flows everywhere the light is not—across every bone and sinew, surrounding every hair. It hugs the shadow within a shadow and, when we are ready, lets down a milky richness white with stars.

We come from the dark, and we return to the dark. We are not merely in it, but *of* it. The darkness does our thinking when we let it, and it is the darkness in which we move.

. . .

APART FROM THE GRAVE, FOOTSTEPS ARE THE BODY'S MOST honest answer to the question of gravity. At night my footfalls are more apparent than they are by light.

Footfall. The word itself seems to carry within it all the quiet of the night.

An ancient Buddhist scripture reminds us, "Light and darkness are a pair, like the foot before and the foot behind in walking." The meaning suggested by the original Chinese words is that daylight is primordially wedded to the night. For the alternation of light and darkness marks not only the passage of day and night, but of the seasons, and the flow of the human soul moving inexorably through time from birth to death to rebirth. Even the planet walks as it rolls from its light to its dark side and back again on its yearly circuit about the sun. The moon, too, walks through its phases. Everything walks—leaves, stones, rivers. Nothing is still.

But most of us nowadays might as well be stationary. From home to work, and from work to home again, we cover the same ground every day. We break the predictability of that sedentary pattern with shopping and trips to the gym and visits with friends and family. And, once or twice a year (if we are lucky), we go on an actual journey and take a vacation . . . which is therapeutic, if only because it restores a sense of the peripatetic to the boring predictability of our lives. But these are all geographical excursions undertaken and examined in the light.

I once saw an injured pigeon in New York City. One of its wings was broken and it could only walk in circles on the pavement. Watching it, I realized that it would probably continue like that until, exhausted, it finally died. There was nothing I could do.

As modern people, we have favored the lit foot of that planetary walking rhythm so much that we are now effectively hobbled by artificial light. It alters our consciousness, and our consciousness reciprocally alters the world. Driven by the illusions of prosperity and progress, we walk the same sad circle from one day to the next, only to die exhausted in the end. Because, after all, how can you get from one day to the next without traveling through the night?

Because we no longer honor the darkness, we have lost touch with the journey of the soul.

. . .

THE ZEN MONASTERY WHERE I TRAINED WAS LOCATED ON A REmote mountain in the Catskills, far from any town or even paved roads. There were no electric lights in any direction. That was what I loved the most about it, although I wouldn't have admitted it at the time. I used to wait until the other monks had turned in for the night. Then I would rise and slip out of the building and take the path around the lake.

There is a very old tradition in Buddhism of meditating at night in the charnel grounds. But my nightly vigils in the monastery graveyard were undertaken without my teacher's supervision. It was outside of my training, and I was careful that no one knew about it. Still, it was what I always had done, and it was what I wanted to do.

I never meditated during those hours or performed austerities or contemplated the impermanence of life. I went to talk to my teacher's teacher, Soen Nakagawa, an old Japanese Zen master I had barely known, but with whom I felt a deep and mysterious connection. I later discovered that he, too, was known for wandering at night.

Soen's ashes were buried beside his *stupa*, a large standing stone with the mantra *Namu Dai Bosa* ("Unite with the Great Bodhisattva") inscribed vertically down the center in Japanese script. On one side of the stupa was a flat stone with his name on it. On the other was the stone of his friend, Nyogen Senzaki, a Japanese monk who had come to America many years before and taught Zen mostly in obscurity. Their graves lay in a small field on the edge of a forest. They might have been lovers in another lifetime to lie so close together in this one.

In any event, they were a pair, like a mother and father, and I poured my heart out to them nightly in the dark.

My wife often speaks to her ancestors late at night. She tells me that Soen and Nyogen are part of the great mandala of ancestral mothers and fathers who have brought us to this moment, handing us down to the mother and father of this lifetime from our mothers and fathers of old.

I only know that they listened to me. Later I might imagine that I was talking to God. But in the beginning I talked to Soen. And I talked to Nyogen. They held me close in the darkness, and they *were* the darkness. They were my first experience in this lifetime of truly knowing and being known.

. . .

ONE DAY ABOUT TEN YEARS AFTER I LEFT THE MONASTERY, A friend who shared my curiosity about spiritual matters introduced me to the teachings of Rebbe Nachman of Breslov, a nineteenth-century Hasidic rabbi whose words seemed to describe the experiences I had been having in the dark since I was a boy. He gave me a small book called *Outpouring of the Soul*, a compilation of the Rebbe's essential teachings on prayer.

Following ancient tradition, Rebbe Nachman advised his disciples to rise for an hour of solitary prayer each night, the object of which was talking alone with God, preferably in a forest or a field. Rebbe Nachman told his followers to speak to God freely, in their own language, about every aspect of their lives, "as though to a true, good friend." He insisted that this unstructured "outpouring of the soul" was the oldest form of meditation, predating all other religious observances, including the daily prayer service and other cornerstones of Jewish liturgy. He once said to his disciples, "Behold! I am taking you on a new path, which is really the old path, the path traveled by our ancient ancestors."

The Rebbe explained the theory behind these solitary vigils with a metaphor he called "Bypassing the Bandits." He compared the daylight world of traditional religious observances to a public highway traveled by many people. "Murderers and robbers lurk there all the time waiting for the unwary, because they know the road. But when a person goes on a new path that is as yet unknown, they are not there to ambush him."

Rising to pray in the darkness was a way of recovering the soul's path through life. It was a way of regaining that inner paradise that was constantly being stolen from us by the fears and anxieties of daily life.

·   ·   ·

Before I attempted to recover that Eden on my own, I visited with three young Breslover Hasidic rabbis. They accepted my presence cheerfully in their small book-lined shul in Monsey, New York, despite the fact that I had arrived unannounced wearing shorts, sunglasses, and a red Hawaiian shirt. Still, they had a difficult time understanding why I was there.

"The Rebbe's teachings on meditation show us how to be good Jews," one of them explained. "That's what they are for."

"That may be," I replied. "But I don't want to become Jewish. Is it possible to follow the path the Rebbe spoke of even if I have no desire to become a Jew?"

I could see the young man undergoing some kind of fierce inner struggle, but in the end a cool head prevailed. He wasn't sure, he confessed. He and his friends were still young and had only recently become rabbis. "You'd better write to a rabbi in Jerusalem," he finally advised.

Instead of writing, that very night I found myself standing in a grassy field a quarter mile from my house, sheltered by a vast dome of stars. I wasn't sure what I was supposed to say. I had long since lost the Christian beliefs of my upbringing, and I was far from Soen's and Nyogen's graves. I didn't know whom I was supposed to be talking to. But somehow it didn't matter. Such questions made sense by daylight. They became irrelevant in the dead of the night with no reference point but the galaxy and the beating of a single human heart.

And so I talked, pouring out all of my dreams and hopes,

fears and anxieties, one after another until, at some elusive point in the process, I knew that I was done. Because I was silent, and God was silent, and a comforting, softly glowing quiet . . . that was not quite sleep and not quite waking . . . was the only thing that remained.

                              .   .   .

BY THE TIME I FINALLY GOT AROUND TO CONTACTING THE RABBI in Jerusalem, I had spent three years doing the practice on my own. He asked how I had come upon the teachings of Rebbe Nachman, given that I wasn't Hasidic, or even Jewish, and I explained about my discovery that the Hour of the Wolf was really the Hour of God. He listened patiently, and corroborated my experiences. But at the end, when I asked for his advice, he was honest: "I have no idea how to guide someone who isn't a Jew. I don't think the Rebbe ever thought of that. Now you really *are* on the road with no bandits—and no other people either. Perhaps, in his mercy, God will show you a way."

As a spiritual practice, *hitbodedut* (or "self-seclusion") lies at the very midpoint between the prehistoric and the modern mind. The Rebbe taught:

> The best time for meditation is at night, when everyone is asleep. Ideally, you should go to a place outside the city and follow a solitary path where people don't even go during the day. . . . When a man goes out to the meadows to pray, every

blade of grass, every plant and flower all enter his prayers
and help him, putting power and strength into his words.

It occurred to me that the subjects in Wehr's studies had
accessed a state of mind that had evolved in human beings
long before they had religion. Absent the demands of urban
living—and the massive agricultural efforts necessary to sustain it—they didn't require anything like an organized system
of religious ritual, practice, and belief. They lived lightly on
the Earth in comparison with modern human beings, moving
in small bands from place to place without ever accumulating
the kinds of property, real or intellectual, that would require
maintenance or protection. They lived in harmony with the
shifting cycles of the seasons, ruled by a consciousness that was
itself rooted in the daily ebb and flow of light. Their experience of life was anchored in those primal rhythms, and so was
their experience of God. Paradise was never lost to them, because paradise was never a place to begin with. Eden was por-
table. Eden was a state of mind.

Rebbe Nachman's advice to his disciples reflected an intuitive understanding of all this. Had he lived another half century to see it, he would doubtless have rejected the theory of
evolution, just as he rejected most other intellectual fruits of
the Enlightenment. And yet, he seemed to understand two
things about human beings that have been true from the very
start: To connect with God, we first have to connect with nature, and to connect with nature, we have to awaken to the
dark. That is why he advised his disciples to follow a solitary

path into the darkness outside the city, and to enlist the aid of plants and flowers once they got there. To follow nature and return to nature—that itself was the path to God.

.   .   .

THERE ARE UNSEEN DIMENSIONS AT PLAY IN ALL OF OUR LIVES, and the darkness allows us to touch and feel those dimensions— and sometimes hear them as well.

Recently the barred owls have become insistent that I come out to walk with them. On nights when I get to bed too late and don't get up to pray, these moody, talkative shadows glide into our yard, sometimes two or three of them at a time, and complain. They trill and hoot as if they were saying, "You'd better get your priorities straight—because we're here to help you, but we can't do all the work."

On my nightly walks I have seen bears and bobcats, rac- coons and coyotes, but my most meaningful encounters have been with owls.

Those great silent hunters have sailed so close to my head that I felt the breeze from their bodies on my face. And unlike most other winged creatures, with the notable exception of the catbird, they are great conversationalists by night. I have had owls speak to me, in their chittering whooing hooting voices, from as close as a yard or two away, just to make acquaintance with a fellow traveler of the night.

Once a great horned owl struck up a conversation with me, there being no other listeners about. WHO *who-who-who*

WHO, he boomed from the tree a few dozen yards from the road. Like the disciple Peter called by Jesus to step from the boat onto the water, I stepped into the darkness under the trees where I knew there must be holes and gullies. There was enough breeze to part the hemlock branches, however, letting the moonlight through, and so at intervals I was able to step closer to the tree in which he stood. I never saw him, but he spoke to me of deep matters for half an hour or more.

. . .

WHAT IS TO BECOME OF US? THAT IS THE QUESTION WAITING for us in the dark.

We don't really have the answer. We have beliefs and hopes, but we don't have any knowledge of the world to come. We only know that we were born, and that we will die. And that the time we have left is steadily shrinking . . . with each passing day . . . with each heartbeat . . . with every breath we take. Our time can only run out.

It makes us upset. It makes us panic.

And so we cry inwardly, *What is to become of us!* It isn't really a question.

But the night answers only, *Who . . . ? Who . . . !*

We all carry the question in the deepest part of our being. We turn on the lights, power up our brains, and fill every crack and crevice with illumination and distraction. But in what shadows remain, there is still that question, waiting for us. Death is waiting for us. Paradoxically, the less space we allot to it, the larger it grows. Perhaps that is why so many of us fear the dark.

· · ·

WHAT IF THERE IS NO LIGHT AT THE END OF THE TUNNEL? What if we die in the darkness and there is *only* darkness, with no sunrise at the end?

What if, when we die, we are forsaken—lost, forgotten, and alone? Worse yet, what if there is no one even to forsake us?

At bottom, our fear of the dark is really the fear of being alone. Children do not naturally fear darkness. They are taught to fear it by modern parents who place them in a crib by themselves. They wake crying in the dark, not because they are afraid of it, but because they are *alone* in it. Bring a child to bed with you and they will nearly always stop crying right away. That is because they belong with their mother and father. They know this. We all know it. Even as adults, we belong with our mothers and fathers in the dark.

There is no more fear once we understand this. There is no loneliness once we realize that the whole world and everything in it is mothers and fathers as deep as the dirt beneath our feet. The whole planet is nothing but mothers and fathers—of every possible species—who have passed before us into the dark. And we ourselves are no one but those very mothers and fathers come back into the light.

Everything that is born will someday die, and all that has died will come to life again. That is the rhythm of the universe.

Call it birth, death, and resurrection. Or call it the workings of a planetary ecology in which nothing can be added or taken away. It amounts to the same truth in the end. Light follows darkness, and darkness follows light.

But it's been centuries since human beings remembered that. We are not alone in the dark.

. . .

FOR MUCH OF MY LIFE I DOUBTED THE EXISTENCE OF AN AFTER-life. There was no world beyond this world, I reasoned. Oddly enough, I somehow still managed to believe in reincarnation. But that wasn't the same as believing in an invisible world. Then, one night as I was walking alone in the falling leaves, I knew suddenly that heaven was real. It was one of those moments when the veil is very thin.

That world. And this world.

Some people believe that the world of the living and the world of the dead are the same — that you don't go anywhere but the ground when you die. If you want to visit the dead, they insist, you have only to go to a graveyard. But don't expect them to notice. Because they can't. Whatever became of their spirit is anyone's guess — if they ever had one. Their bodies are in the ground.

But that has not been my experience.

That world and this world are not the same, but they are connected. The difficulty that most modern people have with the idea of an afterlife (and *most* modern people have a prob-

lem with it, even those who "believe") is that they no longer
have any reliable access to the nonphysical realm. And that has
everything to do with electrical lighting and our modern habit
of staying up so late that our bodies have no choice but to sleep
straight through the night.

At the conclusion of his groundbreaking sleep study,
Thomas Wehr reached a conclusion that, on its surface, seems
more appropriate to a Jungian analyst than a psychobiologist.
Reflecting on the gap of quiet wakefulness experienced by all
of his subjects, he wrote:

> It is tempting to speculate that in prehistoric times this ar-
> rangement provided a channel of communication between
> dreams and waking life that has gradually been closed off
> as humans have compressed and consolidated their sleep.
> If so, then this alteration might provide a physiological ex-
> planation for the observation that modern humans seem to
> have lost touch with the wellspring of myths and fantasies.

Because he was a scientist and not a shaman, such language was probably as close as Wehr could get to saying out-
right that we have lost our access to the realm of the
ancestors—that we can no longer commune with the dead.

Many people today will say that they believe in heaven.
But among modern people such beliefs are usually very shallow. A life of comfort and vacuous self-gratification does little
to invoke the power of belief. Heaven is real when life is real,
and these days it rarely is.

Most of us believe our lives will be real when we have

shone enough light on them, but that is not the case. The more light—the more focused and rapt our attention—the more we send the shadows flying, and the less we feel alive. What we do to our bodies with antibiotics, we do to consciousness with light.

Our souls have become sterile. What was once the realm of the ancestors is now seen only as the grave. In killing the darkness, we have closed the channel that once gave human beings their principal contact with the world beyond.

But it is time to open it again.

Part II

A DARK MANIFESTO

LOOK UP INTO THE SKY ON A STARRY NIGHT AND YOU WILL SEE that there is a lot of darkness in the universe and very little light. So great is the darkness, in fact, that we must find creative ways to measure it. The distance between stars is calculated in light-years, but in reality that convention is a mathematical trick designed to make the mind think that it can grasp the distances involved. We can't really conceive of that much darkness.

So great is the invisible counterweight of darkness in the universe that we think nothing of chipping away a bit of it to make a little something more for ourselves. But we have been chipping away at it with various forms of artificial illumination for a very long time now, and the chips have added up.

When we consider the gentle glow of firelight, it is difficult for us to imagine what a remarkable change it was for early humans to be able to burn wood or pitch or tallow to chase the darkness away. Compared to the light of even a laptop screen, such a flickering, inconstant illumination does not seem very dramatic. But it changed everything about the way our minds and bodies functioned.

Estrogen and testosterone production bumped upward when early humans brought firelight inside of their caves, convincing their bodies that the days were actually growing longer and that it was time to mate. Human females (who were then most fertile in late summer, when food was plentiful) gradually became capable of reproducing at any time of year.

These changes didn't happen overnight (or not literally, at any rate). It wasn't until the agricultural revolution some ten to twelve thousand years ago that they resulted in a dramatic uptick in the global population of our species. But the changes were decisive nevertheless. Nothing in human history before or since compares with the discovery of fire. It literally "lit up" the body and mind, making the course of future human history a foregone conclusion from a biological point of view.

There is no coincidence in the fact that, in the myth of Prometheus, it is the gift of fire that catalyzes human culture. With the potential for year-round human fertility came the implicit feeling that human beings ought to be more fertile—that they ought to command a more prominent place in the ecosystem than before. God's first commandment to humans in the Bible is "Be fruitful and multiply." For God himself is a Promethean figure whose first act is creating light. Before fire, human beings were one species among many—a persistent thread in the evolutionary tapestry that spread here and there through the big picture—but they weren't the *point* of that picture. There was no sense that *Homo sapiens* were the end-point of evolution. There was no sense that, having created them, the world (or God) was effectively done with its creative work.

Call it the birth of human ambition, if you will, or the birth of human culture, but with fire and increased fertility came the idea that a human being ought to be more. And with these came the idea that a human being *was* more. Humans *were* the big picture. Nature was only the backdrop for their story, because humans were the point.

Today it is the introduction of agriculture that is most often credited as the spark that ignited human culture. But agriculture was only the expression of a feeling we had been cultivating in ourselves for a very long time already. Agriculture was the fulfillment of an ambition that had first flickered into existence almost a million years before.

And yet how surprised we are to find ourselves faced today with widespread pollution, overpopulation, and global warming. The only surprise is that we find this surprising. Still, until very recently, we could probably have avoided the worst of it. Because in the late nineteenth century something happened that greatly accelerated our decline.

Conservative social critics have sometimes lamented the loss of a religious consciousness in the age of TV, Twitter, and the Internet. But they are coming into the argument far too late in the game. That loss was already inevitable once the incandescent light bulb came into common use. That was the real tipping point that would eventually guarantee the excesses of the twentieth century—from world wars to climate change to the widespread pollution of rivers, lakes, and streams. For all these spring directly from the overflow of human consciousness, for which the flood of light is both the metaphor and the means.

Advances in science, industry, medicine, and nearly every other area of human life and human enterprise resulted from the influx of good, cheap light like nothing the world had ever seen—a brightness never rivaled by oil or gas. The only casualty in the ongoing conquest of night was darkness, a thing of seemingly little value, an absence really, a blank space on the canvas of eternity we could fill up at will. Or so we thought. The time has come to rethink our relationship with darkness and all that it portends.

Because secretly, we all know it is coming—the cataclysmic event that will change our world. Mostly we feel powerless to avoid it. Still, every now and then we rally. Then we recycle, write our congressmen, stage a protest, or say a prayer. Sadly, none of these will affect the outcome. Secretly we know this, too. We know it is coming. And we know there is nothing we can do.

That is the starting point—to know that our current way of life has no future. We are like the addict who can't recover before he hits bottom. Only when he has fallen as far down as he can go does he find the wherewithal to stand on his own two feet again and begin to look around.

* * *

I WOULD LIKE TO ADVANCE A VERY SIMPLE THEORY. THAT THE-
ory states that, from Lower Paleolithic times onward, human
beings have been addicted to artificial light. In the beginning
that addiction was a very mild one. Now it is entering its final
stages as human beings the world over anxiously wait to hit
bottom.

We are addicted to light and all that it symbolizes—
certainty, the supremacy of our own power and our own knowledge, even the belief that all things can be "made clear."
Progress. Power. Perfection. Destiny. We've gotta have 'em—
even if it destroys our world.

The evidence of that life-destroying addiction is everywhere. Sadly, this is impossible for most of us to see. We have
nothing to compare it to. To witness its full scope would require a journey into space. There, at last, we would be able to
see it whole. For there is one thing about Earth that is obvious
from the upper atmosphere—provided you make the journey
at night—and that is the preponderance of unnatural light.

For a million years our ancestors followed a pattern of daily
life ruled almost entirely by the rising and falling of the sun.
Activity began before daybreak, and persisted for a little while
after dark. Fire was the only light. The nights were long but
hardly vacant. Babies would nurse. The fire would be tended.
And later, stories might be acted out or told. If it was cold,
everyone would snuggle. And couples would make love. Each
person, without exception, woke to wonders during the night.
These were the holy hours—the hours of dreams and visions
that would later inform the sacred texts of the world.

We believe the modern world rests on a petroleum plat-form, but really it rests on light. Petroleum merely drives our cars; light drives our consciousness. And what it drives it to is mostly excess—in all its myriad forms.

In the late 1990s, researchers T. S. Wiley and Bent Formby interviewed Thomas Wehr for their book *Lights Out: Sleep, Sugar, and Survival*. They'd spent years studying the modern diabetes epidemic, only to discover that it was the symptom of a much larger and more complex social disease—an affliction that, although it was a million years in the making, had only become deadly with the introduction of modern artificial light. Although they had based much of their book on Wehr's re-search, the interview was a disappointment.

> When we asked Dr. Thomas Wehr, the head of the de-partment studying seasonal and circadian rhythmicity at the NIH [National Institutes of Health] in Washington, whether he felt the public had a right to know that on less than 9.5 hours of sleep at night—i.e., in the dark—they will (a) never be able to stop eating sugar, smoking, and drinking alcohol and (b) most certainly develop one of the following conditions: diabetes, heart disease, cancer, infertility, men-tal illness, and/or premature aging, he said, "Well, yes, they do have a right to know. They should be told; but it won't change anything. Nobody will ever turn off the lights."

According to the authors, human beings once consumed carbohydrates only in season. Beginning sometime in mid-summer, they would "fatten up" on plant sugars in preparation for the winter, during which time such foods would become very scarce. Women in particular would put on enough fat to carry them through pregnancy—which, in Lower Paleolithic times, would always begin in late summer. The trigger for this all-you-can-eat carbo-fest was more hours of light. People naturally craved the fat-building carbohydrates that were available during that time of year.

With the innovation of campfires about one million years ago, however, our ancestors began to drift from their evolutionary niche as hunter-scavengers and gatherers. It took almost a million years to get there, but eventually they arrived at agriculture, which allowed them to consume carbohydrates at any time of year. This, in turn, made them fertile all year long and substantially increased the number of human beings who could live in close contact with one another, thus inventing cities . . . and culture.

Today we live in a state of perpetual hunger—for food, for sex, and for stimulants of all kinds—because our bodies are convinced that it is August every day of the year and there's no way to convince them otherwise. The mind can scream "Slow down! It's March, don't eat so much" as loud as it wants and it just doesn't matter because the body is responding directly to light, the master switch for all hormone production. The body "knows" from its photoreceptor cells that it's time to eat and mate like there's no tomorrow if it wants to pass its genes on to the next generation.

No one can argue with the body about this as long as we leave the lights on after it gets dark outside. Wiley and Formby only told people what their cells knew already, even though their minds were committed to denying its reality: that the body is the ultimate bottom line.

Ninety-nine percent of all Americans today live in areas that are officially "light polluted," which means that the night is at least ten times brighter than it should be. The world gets more light-polluted by the second, and that means that our bodies are polluted with it, too. At this point, we're actually addicted to that pollution. We're so convinced we have to have it that it's difficult even for experts like Thomas Wehr, who know better, to imagine that it could ever be any other way.

We can, perhaps, imagine a rustic cabin to retreat to for a week once or twice a year. But how many of us would be willing to rely on the dawn to wake us and the dusk to put us to bed when we got there? How many of us would be ready to forgo our phones or computers for a week?

And so what, even if we *were* willing? What are such trips anyway, other than a novelty—a way of roughing it to show we can do without modern conveniences if we have to? They aren't the same as learning permanently to do without. I am reminded of a famous experiment recommended in the book *Alcoholics Anonymous*. It was designed to help someone determine whether they were an alcoholic or not. The experiment was simple: to see if you could go without alcohol for a year. If you could do it, there was little chance you were an alcoholic. Most people who read the book failed after less than a day.

The point is, we don't know how powerful a stimulant artificial light is—far more powerful than nicotine or caffeine—until we have tried to give it up for an extended period of time. And very few of us are capable of doing that without falling hopelessly out of sync with the modern world. When everyone is addicted, there is little logic in recovery—even when the alternative is the personal doomsday scenario offered by Wiley and Formby . . . or the broader cultural end-times that result from a human consciousness that has jumped its evolutionary groove and seized the reins of the world.

So what does that addiction look like now that it has entered its final stage? Can we sober up as a species—or will we go over the edge and crash?

.   .   .

AT A PRESS CONFERENCE IN APRIL 2009, CHIEF WHITE HOUSE science advisor John Holdren described the impending catastrophe of global warming with an ominous metaphor: "We're driving in a car with bad brakes in a fog and headed for a cliff. We know for sure that cliff is out there. We just don't know exactly where it is."

As Holdren explained to reporters, the fog is our uncertainty about climate change and where we stand in relationship to it—whether it is here already or still to come. The cliff is the tipping point beyond which all efforts to forestall disaster are probably pointless. And the bad brakes are inadequate controls and regulations on greenhouse-gas emissions. The car, presumably, is us—America, specifically, and humanity in general—about to go over the edge.

Holdren's metaphor communicates a sense of urgency and peril in language virtually anyone can understand. Nevertheless, something is missing, and that missing something is precisely what makes it a riddle rather than a metaphor.

Strangely, it isn't a riddle that Holdren knows the answer to. He doesn't even realize that he is asking it. That is what makes it so absurd. Because while he mentions the car, the brakes, the fog, and the cliff, nowhere does he mention the road. And the road is the only detail that matters.

How did we end up on a road leading to a cliff?

Was this where we were headed all along—toward the extinction of one half of Earth's plant and animal species by century's end? Were human beings always destined to go over the edge, or was there once another road, and somehow we got off of it?

Few people today believe we should return to the days before agriculture—or that we can, given what we've done to the land and how many of us there are living on it. For now, all we know is that we have to get off the road we're on. In fact, metaphorically speaking, we may have to dispense with roads altogether. We may need to return to the idea of a footpath, rather than a doomed superhighway through time.

.   .   .

LET THERE BE DARKNESS.

The last true revolutionary act left to human beings in the twenty-first century is to turn out the lights. Other acts are possible—acts we may *call* revolutionary—but they do not meet the criteria of the word as it must necessarily be interpreted today. Nothing short of turning out the lights will lead to an overturning of the endgame global system that now has us in its thrall.

To turn out the lights is to turn *over* the human mind—to overthrow it, as it were, so that we can get some perspective on what we truly want and need, so that we can realize that human consciousness is not the sine qua non of reality. That it perceives only the narrowest bandwidth and the smallest part of what is. I say that darkness is the last revolutionary act because it is the only act that effectively overturns human consciousness. And that is the only thing worth revolting against. Consciousness is the problem underlying all others, which, if it is not addressed, will only continue to manifest further problems—one after another—until it has completely destroyed our world.

But all this must seem so heady. So let me make it simple.

It is not necessary to understand anything to join the Dark Revolt. One may even *lead* it and know nothing. Only one step separates us from this revolution. It is as simple as a light switch, as radical as living off the grid.

What is electricity but an exercise in human self-importance? It accomplishes nothing else. It does no good for nature, it is not required for any function the world itself per-forms. What little electricity the world requires it makes itself cheaply and with no pollution.

We speak of "electric lighting" merely because it is impos-sible to separate the two words in our mind. The first power companies were called light companies because light was the principal commodity electricity produced. Only later was it used to power the many machines and gadgets that virtually define our lives today. Even now the primary purpose of electricity the world over is to produce light. All else follows from this. Our other desires all have their origin in light. Light is the father of desire. A mother would not have needed so much illumination for her work, since it is the work already being done by the world.

The Dark Revolt is simple because it cannot be diverted or co-opted. It cannot be used for anything *but* the Dark Revolt. And the revolution itself will follow naturally from this singular act of conscience.

When you turn out the lights in your home or office or apartment, you are making a statement of such startling symbolic power that virtually everything that would need to be included in an ecological or economic or political manifesto is fully included therein. The Dark Revolt leaves nothing and no one out.

But what is the Dark Revolt a revolt *against*? I have said human consciousness, but that is only partly right. It is the *overflow* of consciousness that the Dark Revolt seeks to turn back and overthrow. It does not mean darkening the day. We don't shut out the sun. It means acknowledging a balance much older than we remember. It means a return to time as we once knew it, not time as we know it now.

The time we once knew was marked off in shades of darkness and light. It was in the position of the sun or of the shadows on the ground. We may still have glimpses of that time today. They are commemorated by those quaint words *dawn* and *dusk*, which mean so little to us now when either can be obliterated at the flick of a switch.

Darkness is the one remaining revolutionary act. Changing the political order does not matter. Economies are all more or less alike. Governments and cultures rise and fall. The person who chooses to turn off the lights and lie awake in darkness embraces the truth of a life before and beyond all of these. The only way back to the path we once traveled on as a species is through the darkness of deep time.

·   ·   ·

TURN OUT THE LIGHTS—AND LEAVE THEM OFF—AND WE WILL experience a consciousness our minds have never known but our bodies still remember. Leave them on, and it scarcely matters what else we do or leave undone. We will not significantly alter our path through time. Nor will we alter the path of our species, which has taken a collective detour leading nowhere but oblivion and extinction. We persist perpetually in making all of this seem more complicated than it is.

Turn off the news. Forget Facebook and Twitter. Don't read the paper. Let the world turn and the seasons pass on their own. Then wake up in the middle of the night a year later and ask yourself if anything is amiss. If so, let go of more media. Let go of more light. Wake again and ask if anything is lacking. Repeat as necessary until you have remembered what it means to be a person, because this is the one thing everyone forgets.

What is it we have forgotten as a species that allows us to wreck the planet? People look everywhere for the answers to this question except for the place where it is to be found. We are like the drunk searching for his car keys under a streetlamp because the light is better there. We can't find our souls in the daylight, since we lost them in the night.

Turn off the lights and leave them off, and after a few weeks you will discover something miraculous. When the sun goes down, your mind will grow quiet. All the things that were supposed to be important—the things you fretted over, the ones that kept you up at night making you feel trapped, faced with impossible trade-offs—all these fade as though the plug has been pulled on them. In fact, the plug has been pulled.

Claim your place in the dark and the body takes over, solving problems the mind could not, making all things simple that are made complicated by light. The bad choice. The false ambition. The things society would compel us to value which, absent the thousand-watt voltage of an artificially illuminated world, are revealed for the destructive illusions they really are. Turn off the lights and leave them off and, in short, you remember who you are.

· · ·

Would you like me to provide an argument in favor of all of this in order to convince you? Should I acknowledge the wondrous advances of human reason, the medical milestones, the household conveniences, and the steady march of progress, all of which we will surely lose in the dark? I will not make that argument or concede those points. There is no argument you will listen to that will embolden you to drop this

superlit illusion of modern life. You have to come to the deci-
sion on your own.

There will be those who seek to drag me into the light,
make me stand and deliver and defend myself. But this I will
not do. There is no reason for it. The stars are my argument.
My witness is the moon. Remain plugged in if you wish, but
when the darkness comes—your death and the decline of our
species—don't complain that you can't see by it. Don't say,
"The world has gone dark and now I am as one made blind."

. . .

FOR ME, PRAYER STARTED WHEN I WAS A CHILD. BUT AS A TEEN-
ager I became confused and gave it up. Or perhaps I only
poured my childhood prayers into walking, because I walked a
lot. When I became a Buddhist and learned to chant and to
meditate, I was praying again, but I never loved it. Except for
the time I spent in the graveyard with Nyogen and Soen when
I was a monk. That I loved.

Each night at dusk in the monastery, we would gather in
the meditation hall, lit by a single candle, to chant the lineage
of names from my teacher's teacher all the way back to the
Buddha. There were eighty-one names in all—twenty-seven
teachers had lived in India, twenty-seven in China, and twenty-
seven in Japan. Soen's name was the last on the list, and because I had known him, he was my point of contact with them
all.

Zen is a patriarchal religion, and so all of these ancestors

were male. But I learned in the graveyard that something surprising happens to a man when he passes back into darkness
from the light. The pride of power and the authority of
gender—all of these disappear when we die. We become
smooth and shell-like on an ocean of time, through which we
tumble from lifetime to lifetime, sometimes male and sometimes female, but endowed spiritually with the depth and wisdom of both. The soul's journey is a beginningless odyssey, and
the dead remember it all.

Sometimes children remember it, too.

When my daughter was four years old, she overheard my
wife and me discussing an article about early man. She begged
to learn more and that Saturday I took her to the library, where
we found a book that described the 3.2-million-year-old *Australopithecus* skeleton found in Ethiopia in 1974 that anthro-
pologists named Lucy, after a Beatles song. In the way that very
young children will, Sophie conceived an unshakable desire
to see Lucy.

She decided Lucy resided at the American Museum of
Natural History in New York, which we had once lived near,
and nothing would convince her otherwise. I tried to tell her
that Lucy lived in a museum in Ethiopia, but she would not be
dissuaded from her belief. Finally, I gave in and drove her two
hours to the museum, knowing that we would find only dino-
saur fossils and perhaps a few dioramas from prehistoric times.
But I was wrong.

As it turned out, there was a traveling exhibition on early
man, and when we went to the museum, there at the entrance
to the exhibit was Lucy in a case against a wall. Or perhaps it

was a replica. It hardly mattered. Sophie flew across the crowded room and pressed her whole body against the glass. "Lucy!" she cried. "I came. I came."

Later, we made our usual trip to the gift shop and Sophie announced that she wanted to buy a stuffed toy of Lucy to take home as a memento. I had to explain to her that the museum, which had stuffed toys of all kinds of creatures, including dinosaurs, wouldn't have one of Lucy. Lucy had lived so long ago, I told her, that now she was only bones. Sophie looked at me disbelievingly and insisted that we return to the exhibit, where she stood still for a full minute facing the partially reconstructed skeleton of this 3.2-million-year-old girl, no bigger and no smaller than she was. Finally, she stepped forward and laid her hand gently upon the glass and whispered, "Good-bye, Lucy."

When we returned home that night, my wife asked her if we'd seen Lucy, and Sophie said that we had, "but now she is only bones."

She said it for me. I could tell she didn't believe it. It wasn't what she had seen.

Behind us are the dead, in numbers as vast as the distances between stars. And the dead are beneath us, too—in soil and sediment, reaching down into the very bedrock. Dig as deep as you can and the dead are there already. The history of our planet is nothing but a history of the dead.

But it isn't a dead history. Because the dead are still there in the dark. They are only waiting to be acknowledged. Their voices speak in the language of dreams, or through the owls or fireflies. They speak through the weather, and stir briefly, like a breeze at the window, in the spaces that open between thoughts in the middle of the night.

And yet, how few of us know anything about our direct ancestors of only a few generations ago. My Zen lineage went back 2,500 years to the time of Shakyamuni Buddha, but that is nothing set against the backdrop of evolutionary time. Every plant and animal cell on the planet is the result of an unbroken biological lineage going back to the beginning of all life. And even *that* beginning had another beginning. The Earth, the Sun, the Moon: all have ancestors. Even our universe — the mother of a hundred billion galaxies — must surely have had a mother and father of her own.

But to grasp even the smallest part of all this (and it only requires a small part) involves ways of knowing that rarely venture into the light. The dead are in the dark.

. . .

THE DEAD ARE IN THE DARK IN NUMBERS TOO VAST FOR OUR ordinary consciousness to comprehend. Who are they? They are more than our lineage of direct biological ancestors, as numberless as those ancestors are. And they aren't just human. Every plant, animal, and insect alive on the planet today is linked to ancestral mothers and fathers without end. And every cell has ancestors, too. Even the mountains and valleys and deserts, the streams and the oceans, have ancestors. Everything that exists now exists because of what has come before.

But "before" doesn't mean gone.

Nothing comes or goes—least of all Life in all its myriad forms, corporeal or insubstantial, in awaketime or in dreamtime. The dead wait just beyond the veil. They occupy that mythic, primal place we can only access from the world of dreams or in that numinous space that opens in the dark. Call them ancestors, call them the dead. Spirits, ghosts, angels, fairies, devas—whoever or whatever they are now, they can see us and sense us from the dark. They follow everything we do, even if our super-illuminated world, and the hyper-lit consciousness it fuels, make it impossible for us to experience them.

The dead are the Army of the Dark Revolt. And they are waiting for the living to lead them. But if we can't—or *won't*—then they will lead themselves. For if we cannot solve our problems on our own, they will solve them for us. Nature will solve them for us. The planet remembers secrets that science can scarcely conceive of. The dead remember it all.

We strut about for our hour in the sun as if we are free and independent of that great reality we once called Mother and Father but now can understand only through distant, disembodied terms like *planetary ecosystem*. But we are not free of it. We are not independent. Everything is connected. The living go on living from one moment to the next . . . only because of the dead.

All time is ancestral time. We stand atop Mothers and Fathers without end. Waking up in the dark helps us to remember that great reality, and helps us to remain connected to it once we do.

. . .

WHEN I SPEAK OF ANCESTRAL TIME, I AM NOT TALKING ABOUT time as we normally experience it. Not clock time or calendar time. Not the time it takes a falling object to reach terminal velocity, nor the time for a loan to mature. I am not speaking of time that "waits for no man," or time that "flies." The problem we face on the edge of the cliff is BIG time. Time so big it dwarfs history. Time so vast that all human memory could vanish into it and scarcely a ripple would remain. Deep time.

We know it is there—at our back—but we don't know what to do with it. It frightens us. It gives us vertigo. If we feel alone in the dark, we feel terrifyingly isolated and lost in the enormity of deep, dark time.

If we compare the span of our lives to the few thousand years of recorded (a better word might be *illuminated*) human history, it fits comfortably inside. A bit loosely perhaps, like a marble rolling around inside of a shoe box. Still, it makes a kind of sense. Compare that life-span to the age of the planet, however, and suddenly we can't feel the walls of that box anywhere near us. We can't even see them in the distance. Our marble can roll forever and never touch the wall. Suddenly we have no idea where—or even *when*—we are.

Time is a big problem for human beings and the reason is simple: We can find no home in it. We can't figure out where we belong. This has been the central problem of human life since the inventions of agriculture and written record keeping, when we first lost touch with our ancestors. It's the reason we feel so driven to be fruitful and multiply, filling the world with more and more people, until it seems that the world was made *only* for people—as if having as many people in it as possible were the point.

But that is not the point. It never was.

Lost in time, we have surrounded ourselves with ourselves, with nothing but human beings and human culture to define us. At seven billion and growing, we've made a snug fit for ourselves in the world. We can't fill the "box" of deep time, but we can fill the world so full of human culture that scarcely anything else can fit in—not even ourselves in the end. Are we mad? Or only lonely for the ancestors who once addressed our deepest concerns? The ones who answered our panicked query "Where am I?" with the only true answer the universe has ever known: "You are not alone."

*   *   *

REBBE NACHMAN ONCE TOLD THE STORY OF A KING AND HIS prime minister, who was also his good friend. The king told the prime minister, "I see by the stars that everyone who eats from this year's grain harvest is going to go mad. What do you think I should do?"

The prime minister suggested they set aside a portion of good grain so that they would not have to eat from the tainted wheat. But the king objected, "There will not be enough for everyone, and if only we two eat from the good wheat, everyone will be insane but us. They will look at us and say that we are the mad ones. No. What we must do is this. We, too, shall eat from the tainted grain, but we will each place a sign on our head. I will look at your forehead, and you will look at mine, and when we see the sign, at least we will remember that we are mad."

Rebbe Nachman was a Hasidic Jew, and so the "sign" he is referring to can only be the *tefillin*, small leather boxes containing scriptural parchments that are worn on the arm and forehead by observant Jews during prayer.

Nearly everyone who hears this story appreciates its melancholy humor. And yet, it is such an odd story. For if the *tefillin* are meant to remind Jews that they have been delivered from a world gone mad, according to the story that doesn't make them sane. If anything, it confirms their madness. The message is paradoxical: They live in a world within a world, which they call Judaism. But that world is also mad. The only difference is that its inhabitants can recognize their madness by reading its sign in another. The other is a mirror of the self.

As a curious footnote to the story: Jewish women do not wear *tefillin*—which could mean either that they simply do not have the same rights as men, or that they do not need quite so much reminding . . . or perhaps both. They know instinctively that the world is crazy, and that men have made it that way.

Just how crazy are we—those of us reading this, and me writing it—in the opening decades of the millennium? The following may give us some idea.

Type the words "population curve" into Google Images and click on the first item that pops up and you will find a Wikipedia graph charting the growth of the subspecies *Homo*

sapiens sapiens over a small but decisive portion of its extremely long history—the period from the dawn of agriculture
down to the present day. It's like watching the slow burn of a
long fuse as it inches toward the bomb.

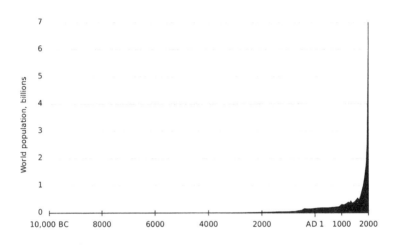

For nine thousand years the line hugs the bottom of the
graph, indicating a world population still measured in the
lower millions. Then, about the time of the Axial Age, when
the great philosophies and religions are being born, it suddenly
rises to 100 million. Over the thousand years that follow, it
doubles, and then doubles again, rising steadily from there
until the time of the Industrial Revolution, at which point it
tops a billion. Then it goes straight up.

Returning to Rebbe Nachman's story, we can say that for a
long time the grain mostly worked. There were inequities in
the way it was distributed, and plenty of wars were fought over
who got what and how much. But it wasn't poison. Then something started to go wrong. Fueled by the fantasy of limitless

progress and soaring prosperity, two things happened simultaneously: The wheat went bad, and there was more of it than ever before.

We are, of course, now deep in the land of metaphors. But in this case metaphors can accomplish something that facts alone cannot.

Al Gore's Academy Award–winning 2006 film *An Inconvenient Truth* set forth the facts of climate change, including PowerPoint graphs showing the rise in global temperatures and CO_2 emissions since the Industrial Revolution. Gore demonstrated convincingly the one-to-one correlation between these and the rise in human population and the use of fossil fuels, displaying a chart virtually identical to the Wikipedia graph.

Despite the claims of Gore's critics that he had exaggerated the risks and exploited the widespread fear of global warming to his own political advantage, when pushed to defend their positions, even his detractors had to concede that his numbers were generally accurate. Exit polls for the film showed an overwhelmingly positive response, even in politically conservative communities, with an overall approval rating of 92 percent.

But where did that information go? Did the facts of global warming, displayed with blazing clarity by a former U.S. vice president, actually convince anyone that they were mad?

Obviously not. The film came and went. People saw it. They panned it or praised it. Then they went on with their lives. In a world where everyone is mad, there is little point in recovering one's sanity. You can assemble the facts and write them large. You can put them on posters and billboards, on the Internet and the nightly news. You can debate them forever, and even *win* the debate, and it just doesn't matter in the end. It's all media. It's all talk. It's all just endless light.

There are truths that can only be learned in the dark.

· · ·

In a dream I am outside with a group of men and women standing around a large cooking pot. I am hungry and want to eat. But I am curious about where the meat in the pot has come from. That is when I notice that each person has cut off one of his or her arms and placed it in the pot. I wonder whether I can bring myself to do this, knowing I must if I want to eat. That is when I awake.

It is hard to emerge from such a dream without questioning your sanity, visions of cannibalism occupying a relatively low place on the scale of normal thoughts and fantasies. But the dream was telling me something, and after a little reflection I realized what it was. The key was a paragraph I had read in an anthology of environmental writing only a day or two before.

In 1972, when the environmental movement was still very much in its infancy, the United Nations convened the world's first international conference to raise awareness about threats to the global ecology. The official report of the Stockholm Conference included a passage that today reads almost like an eco-spiritual creed:

> Life holds to one central truth—that all matter and energy needed for life moves in great closed circles from which nothing escapes and to which only the driving fire of the sun is added. Life devours itself: everything that eats is itself eaten; every chemical that is made by life can be broken down by life; all the sunlight that can be used is used. Of all that there is on Earth, nothing is taken away by life, and nothing is added by life—but nearly everything is used by life, used and reused in thousands of complex ways, moved through vast chains of plants and animals and back again to the beginning.

In other words, we eat . . . and we are eaten. We pay the price for our lives *with* our lives, whether we want to or not. That is because not one of us can stand apart from the matrix of biological blessings that the Earth provides. We don't own those lives any more than we own the planet from which they were taken and to which they must return. We don't even own our arms. That is what makes life holy—the fact that nothing is wasted, that nothing is extra, that nothing can ever be taken away. Everything on Earth belongs to everything else. We are not alone.

Today, when we have drifted so far into theological specu-lation that we are blind to the most basic realities governing the life of our planet, we are apt to miss the real wisdom preserved in our sacred scriptures, even though it is obvious for anyone with eyes to see.

The ritual of the Eucharist, for instance.

Jesus is born in a manger, a feed trough for animals, and tells his disciples on the night before his crucifixion that his body is being broken for them to eat, his blood shed for them to drink. There is no reason for him to tell them this unless it is a teaching—the story of his death and resurrection would work without it, and the various prophecies contained in the Jewish scriptures would still be fulfilled. But he makes a special point of the bread and wine. It is a symbolic ritual. The disciples aren't really being asked to eat his body or drink his blood. But what that ritual represents is nevertheless very real. In fact, it is the realest thing there is.

Jesus's death is not a sacrifice to atone for sin, as the church has long taught—unless eating is a sin in itself. Rather, it is a portrait of life at its most basic level. Whatever eats must be eaten. That is a terrifying prospect as long as we flee from it, but once we submit to it, as Jesus does, there is no more fear.

Once we are born we must eat, taking the lives of plants and animals in order to live. But, then, as is only right, we ourselves are eaten in the end. Some cultures insist on cremation as a way of escaping from this (symbolically, at least), but it doesn't change the basic equation. We make food for other beings our whole lives with our excrement, and insects and microorganisms are constantly feeding off us from the moment we are born. The flora in our intestinal systems alone is composed of an estimated 100 trillion microorganisms, which both eat us and keep us alive. In that respect, the human body is itself a microcosm of the planet, in which everything is constantly consuming everything else in a pattern too varied and complex for anyone to grasp fully but the intelligence of Nature herself.

The communion ritual in Christianity is one of the last symbolic remnants of an older Earth-wisdom that has now been all but lost from the world. Our lives and the planet are one. When Jesus says, "This is my body which is given for you," he is reminding us of the one great universal truth, rather than laying claim to a singular historic event. Every time we eat, we are eating God. And it is God who eats us as well.

Jesus's teachings are filled with ecological metaphors and riddles—with lilies that are saner in their Earth-wisdom than Solomon in all his glory, and seeds that must die in order to be born. Even his resurrection echoes the ancestral teachings of deep time. You can kill him and bury him, but you cannot stop him. The dead and the living are forever trading places in a dance as old as the universe itself. There aren't just Second Comings, but Third and Fourth Comings as well. There is no end to it. The story of salvation doesn't *have* a beginning or end. How could it?

That is what redeems us. That is what makes us "saved." Find spiritual oneness with those great ancestral chains of plants and animals spoken of in the Stockholm Commission report, and you are forever redeemed and brought "back again to the beginning," even if you have no religious beliefs at all. But try to escape from that oneness, and your car can only go over a cliff.

· · ·

OUR FAMILY LIVES IN A HOUSE IN THE WOODS AT THE END OF A long driveway. Often, in the middle of the night, I will walk to the end of it to look at the stars. Once I've reached the road, there are a lot more of them because of the gap in the trees. Sometimes I walk a ways toward town following the flow of the galaxy above my head rather than the road itself, which on moonless nights is so dark I cannot see my shoes.

At the bottom of the hill there is a grassy field that used to belong to horses but now belongs to no one but the sky. About twenty years ago, something terrible happened at the house whose owners the horses belonged to, a large white Victorian with lots of outbuildings and apple trees. But now no one re-members what it was, or they won't say. The house has been empty since, although a single porch light remains on always, 365 days a year.

Someone always replaces the bulb when it burns out, but it's a mystery who this might be. No one comes and no one goes. The house follows the seasons to the accompaniment of that solitary trickle of electric light, falling a little further into ruin with the passing of every year. Somehow it always feels like a metaphor—as if that lone bulb burning through the night were the expression of a sorrow too deep to express in any other way. It seems to gather the sorrows to it. As if, in the dark-ness, they were attracted to its light.

About ten years ago, I began studying a Buddhist scripture

known as the Lotus Sutra. The main point of the sutra is contained in the symbolism of its title. For the lotus is a beautiful white flower that opens in the light at the surface of a pond, though its roots lie deep in the mud and muck below. No mud, no lotus. The dark and the light are one.

The Lotus Sutra reaches its climax when the Buddha explains that life is eternal. But by that he doesn't mean life in some distant heavenlike realm. Life in *this* world is eternal. Living beings seem to come and go like lotus blossoms at the surface of the pond. But the Buddha—the eternal Life Force that abides in each individual being and truly *is* each being— that does not come or go. To his anxious disciples, committed to a linear vision of time and ensnared by the ceaseless drama of gain and loss, he says, "I am always here. I only appear to come and go."

One night before bed, I was reading the chapter from the Lotus Sutra entitled "Emerging from the Earth." In that chapter, the disciples who have gathered to hear the sutra vow to protect and spread its teachings during future ages. Unexpectedly, however, the Buddha tells them that this is unnecessary. There are already innumerable beings who have been placed in charge of preaching and protecting that sutra. When the Buddha has spoken these words, the earth splits open, and out of it emerge "immeasurable thousands, ten thousands, millions of bodhisattvas." Golden in color and endowed with the thirty-two characteristics of enlightened beings, they had previously occupied what the sutra calls "the world of empty space underneath this world in which living beings must struggle and endure." Hearing the voice of the Buddha calling to them, however, at last they have emerged. The Buddha's living disciples are shocked when they see them and cry as one, "How can this be?"

What impressed me about the story was that the disciples knew nothing of the existence of these ancient Earth teachers before the Buddha called them forth. Two millennia ago, when the New Testament and the Lotus Sutra were both being written, that knowledge was already being lost. On a mountain in Judea, and on another in northern India, it was necessary to remind the living of "a new path that is really the old path." The further the living travel into the realm of light and culture, the more they forget the darkness and the dead. And the more they lose their way.

But the vision of the Lotus Sutra was ultimately hopeful for the future. For it spoke of that ancestral path being lost and reclaimed over and over again on its journey through deep time. If, throughout the universe, living beings were always going off a cliff through pride or arrogance—or simply because they forgot who they really were—they were always dusting themselves off after a fall and finding their way forward again, recovering an ancient bodhisattva wisdom that taught them how to live.

As I read the sutra that night, I found myself wondering what its authors would have made of Charles Darwin and Louis and Mary Leakey and the countless "bodhisattvas" who had emerged when they'd first "split open" the earth, recovering the remains of our bygone ancestors, either by inferring their existence from current biology, as Darwin did, or by literally digging them up like the Leakeys. Together with their colleagues and successors, these pioneers of deep history had produced something one might call "The Evolution Sutra," the message of which was identical to that of the Lotus.

Were the creators of the Lotus Sutra alive today, they would probably tell us that we are on the verge of recovering a much longer path through time than we have ever imagined for ourselves before. Did we really suppose that we were on a journey of only a few thousand years in duration, or a few hundred thousand? The wisdom of our ancestors has been passed down, not just from person to person on that journey, but from species to species. Our task now is to recover it again. That teaching is the price of admission to our future as human beings—provided we want that future to be a deep one. The good news is that, according to the Lotus, at many other times and places throughout the vast darkness of the cosmos, that teaching has been lost and recovered before.

I will only add that later that night, when I woke for the Hour of God, the porch light on the abandoned house had burned out again and the sadness I'd felt before had all gone. We may find our way forward as a species or not—and I won't live to see it in any case—but we can recover the old path even now. It opens in the darkness . . . and takes us where it goes.

. . .

EVERY ORGANIZED RELIGION CREATED AFTER THE DAWN OF AG-riculture placed a premium on human destiny. Thus, every religion in the world today, with the exception of those rare outliers among indigenous peoples, was created to answer a question the very asking of which betrays a bias so vast we can scarcely see around it: *What is the meaning of human life?*

Put simply, all religion is anthropocentric. Religion is the product of an age stretching back some ten thousand years that, provided we are someday privileged to evolve beyond it, may be known to some future species of ourselves as the *Anthropocene*—an era when *Homo sapiens* dominated the planet, harnessing its energies to their sole purpose and appropriating its natural resources exclusively for human use.

Waking up in the dark is a way of reaching around the Anthropocene to catch glimpses of what might have existed before it—a time when it was still possible to recognize a human being as part of the landscape of the world, before it became what it is now: a dazzling figure against the ground of nature with such an overwhelming sense of its own destiny that the ground it sprang from is virtually invisible to it now. It is as if it had no backdrop, no context, and no home. As if it were a thing unto itself, glorious, self-determined, and alone.

But it isn't just religion that champions the psychotic indifference of our species to nature—as if our life and the planet were not one. Those archaeologists and evolutionary biologists who challenge the Bible's account of creation rarely challenge with any real enthusiasm the anthropocentric worldview for which the Bible's creation story serves as the founding narrative. They are as much believers as the fundamentalists are. This is what I find tiresome in the writings of neo-atheists. It is a very dull mind indeed that cannot see what is really being created in Genesis. It has nothing to do with the light and darkness, or man and woman, or seven days as opposed to seven million years. What is being created is the sense of a human destiny separate and distinct from this world.

Any culture that takes Genesis as its founding story can only have developed as ours has. The Bible is a thought experiment that shows us what becomes of the species that defines itself apart from nature, imagining a future for itself that is separate from the world's. Revelation is therefore the natural and inevitable end of Eden—the place that story was headed all along. At the end of the Bible, human beings must imagine "a new heaven and a new earth." What has become of the heaven and earth they had before? They have destroyed them.

Today the same narrative gets played out by futurists and science fiction authors who imagine that it is possible for human beings to migrate to other planets when this one becomes overpopulated or destroyed. But this is as much a fantasy as the New Jerusalem was, because even if human beings were capable of escaping to other planets, they could not survive there without their ancestors and their Mother. Evolution hasn't prepared them for it. We can't stray far from those vast closed chains of plant and animal life of which we are an integral part. A human being can only survive for a few minutes without oxygen. It might take a little longer to feel the absence of those trillions of organisms that have traveled with us down the long dark road of evolutionary time inside of our guts— organisms from which we have never for an instant been parted—but the end result would be the same. We might figure out how to eat in space, but if we couldn't figure out how to be eaten, we would die.

We belong to this planet, not to another. Its sunlight is imprinted on our cells. The dirt under our fingernails is our dirt—the Mother we came from, and the Mother to whom we return.

. . .

IT'S STRANGE HOW MUCH MODERN PEOPLE SECRETLY CRAVE weather-related disasters—the blizzard that shuts down a city, bringing travel and commerce to a halt, the tropical storm that knocks out power, leaving millions in the dark. People of earlier centuries rightly feared such events and earnestly prayed to be delivered from them. Now there's an excitement that begins building the moment we hear of such a storm.

That the larger storms sometimes turn deadly does little to chasten our feelings of anticipation. Part of it is the knowledge, gleaned from a century of experience, that things will soon go back to normal. Another is the paradox of media reports, which transform terrible events into a form of nightly entertainment while pretending to inform. In the meantime, provided no one we know has suffered harm, there's some comfort in having nature force our hands. It feels good to release our death grip on the steering wheel, and take up the snow shovel instead.

There's a tension between the part of us that wants to move along at speed, infatuated with our ever-proliferating array of screens and gadgets, and the part of us that deeply hates them, too. There's the part that doesn't want to be bothered with other people's lives and is therefore comfortable with the false proximity that social media affords. But there's also the part that is heartbroken at the loneliness and isolation of the life we are living—the part that requires medication and constant distraction just to endure it. If we can't stop ourselves from embracing the things we secretly hate and know to be bad for us, the question becomes what *will* stop us? Climate change is one answer. The end of oil would be another. In the meantime we have our storms.

It's a relief to have life placed on a real footing again, when it becomes about water and food, warmth and companionship. It's a relief, even if we can't do it for ourselves. Even if it lasts only for an evening or a day.

A few summers ago, as we were nearing the end of our yearly vacation, we heard that a hurricane was headed straight for Cape Cod. With only a day left on the rental house, we decided to make a dash for it rather than take the brunt of the storm. As it turned out, we'd have been better off staying where we were. Because instead of hitting the Cape, the storm struck a hundred miles inland, wiping out parts of the Catskill town just to the north of us and shutting off the power in our community for over a week.

Not only was the whole neighborhood plunged into utter darkness, the whole town was, too. A few people powered up generators, but the pinpricks of light they provided were powerless over that much darkness. There was no way they could prevail against the night.

People grumbled, but you could tell they were secretly delighted. They just didn't have the vocabulary to express it. Few of us know how saturated our minds and bodies are with light. Even fewer realize how profoundly modern media poisons the soul.

The storm brought down huge trees all up and down the road where we live. At night I'd have to climb over them just to complete my walk. I was sad to lose them, but there was something peaceful about the solid bulk of their bodies lying full across the road. The storm had been violent, but it wasn't a human violence. There was no callousness in it. Whatever is born will die, and those trees understood death better than a Buddha. Later they were removed piecemeal with a chainsaw by cutting them into manageable lengths and loading them into the backs of pickups that groaned audibly with the weight.

It was surprising how fast most people adjusted to the longer nights and earlier bedtimes. It was harder to make coffee without electricity, but most people had less need of it anyway. For the first time in months—in some cases, years—they were finally getting enough rest.

Friends who knew of my habit of waking in the dark were suddenly interested in talking with me about it. Some reported strange dreams. A man I barely knew told me, "When the grid goes down, the mythical creatures return." He said it twice, like an incantation. The lit part of my mind dismissed what he was saying, but the dark part knew that it was true.

Our small town drifted together during those weeks, as neighbors who hadn't spoken in years shared meals and news with one another, helping with repairs and errands, and catching up on the hundred details of daily life that people share who live on the same road—or would share if they talked more often. Without phones there was no way to communicate without speaking face-to-face. But just as quickly the town drifted apart again, as people went back to the larger business of the world. The Internet was up, the interstate was open, and the TV came back on.

People's lives went back to normal after the hurricane was over and its devastation had been repaired or removed. But my own life never went back. That was because of something that happened a week before the storm.

One night on Cape Cod a voice woke me at 2 a.m. with the words "If you rise to say the rosary tonight, a column of saints will support your prayer." In all the years I'd been waking up in the dark, I'd never heard a voice. But for all that week and for the twelve days of darkness that followed the hurricane, it woke me every night. I'd have said it had something to do with the darkness if it hadn't started before the storm.

As it was, it made my experience of the hurricane different than it otherwise would have been. I'd always thought of my night walks as solitary time. I always felt happy and content in the darkness. But apart from my encounters with the owls and other animals, I assumed that I was alone in it. Even during the years I'd spent talking to Soen and Nyogen, neither had spoken to me. Later, when I spoke to God, it was the same.

I had no idea what "a column of saints" might refer to. The phrase had a Christian ring. But I felt supported, that much was true. For the first time in my life, I understood that loneliness was an illusion. Not one of us was ever alone. The dark wasn't dark the way an empty jar was when you looked down into it. It was filled to overflowing with "saints."

They weren't saints in the ordinary sense. Ashes to ashes, dust to dust, said the church, as if that were the end of the matter. As if soil and rock and water weren't the holiest things on Earth. The church was insane when it came to bodies and matter—and especially when it came to dirt. But the dead of the planet were saints nevertheless. They were the body and soul of the world.

One night when the trees were finally off the lines and the power was soon to come on, the voice said, "You haven't prayed for anything. Is there nothing you want?"

I thought for a moment. "Only for this," I said.

. . .

THE POINT OF THE DARK REVOLT IS TO DISCOVER A NEW PATH that is really the old path. But in our case the ancestors are a good bit older than the first-century rabbis that Rebbe Nachman had in mind. Our ancestors are *Homo erectus*, *Homo habilis*, *Australopithecus*, and those far older species who stand below us, columnlike and imperturbable, down to the very bottom of time.

I sometimes call that path a "green" one because for millions of years it was sustainable. It was a path with an extremely remote past and—potentially, at least—a remote future as well. But today I worry that most people, if asked what path they are on, will answer that they belong to this or that spiritual tradition (or none at all), while, in reality, the path they are traveling on is about to go over a cliff.

For the first ten thousand years of that ongoing assault on nature we call the "agricultural revolution," this was not so clear. True, we fought over resources, killed one another with impunity, and—always in the name of progress—exterminated whole races of people, animals, and plants. Still, it wasn't obvious that the development of human monoculture was essentially a dead end. It wasn't obvious that repurposing every aspect of the planet for our own benefit wasn't really to our benefit at all. We kept thinking it would work out, even with mounting evidence to the contrary. Shouldn't we have seen this coming? Probably so. But, then, we didn't want to. Who likes to admit it when they're lost?

That older, saner path mapped out for us by nature still exists today. The ancestors are ready to guide us on that journey the instant we resolve to follow it. This is the "straight way" that Jesus spoke of, the narrow footpath that leads from life to death, and from death to life again. To find it, we only have to leave the foggy superhighway we are traveling on, pedal-to-metal without any brakes, content to follow the white dividing line laid down for us without ever pausing to wonder where it goes.

Who will save us? Not our leaders, that much is certain. One commissioner of highways is as bad as another if both are waving us to our doom. Ideologues won't save us. Scientists won't save us. And our premiers and presidents can't even save themselves.

Look! There are burning bushes all around us even now. There are ancestors beyond all reckoning waiting to guide us through the dark. They're all saying the same thing—sometimes in a whisper, sometimes with a scream.

Here is a new path that is really the old path. If you want to survive, take it. If not, then just carry on as you are. It will all be over soon.

I DO NOT REMEMBER WHEN I FIRST INTUITED THAT THE DARK-ness was a woman. Probably I always knew. But I remember the night I knew for sure.

I had risen and dressed for the Hour of God and was stand-ing with my hand on the doorknob, about to leave the house for my walk, when I felt the weight of a hand on my shoulder and a voice said, "Don't go out tonight. Remain calm—and very, very still." This I did, positioning myself lengthwise on the couch beside the downstairs window, looking out on the moon, the darkness, and the stars.

The night was unusually beautiful, the weather just this side of cool. I'd have loved to walk, but I'd heard the voice before—spoken softly, but clearly, in some innermost room of the mind. Some people would be frightened at such a thing, but I never was. Maybe it comes from having spent so much time in the dark. In the dark, *every* voice could be the voice of an ancestor or a spirit guide. In the darkness, who can tell the living from the dead?

I quickly entered a place of such quiet that I cannot remember having any thoughts at all—or at least a state in which the thoughts are so few that you can see them coming, like the traveler you witness crossing an open plain on foot whose approach is visible from a long way off. It was the state one sometimes experiences in those hard-to-describe in-between stages of sleep, except that I was awake.

After about forty-five minutes like this, my breath caught in my throat because someone was there I hadn't seen coming.

I felt a presence directly to my left and opened my eyes. There beside me was a girl about seventeen years old. Her face was pale and moonlike, with a few freckles around her nose. Her eyes were hazel, her auburn hair cut short. Over her mouth someone had placed an X of black electrical tape.

I can tell you to the last particular what her hair and face and eyes looked like—the shape of her mouth and her nose. The glow of her face, which seemed lit by something like candlelight, although the room was completely dark. But if I did that, you might still imagine her as a vision.

Was she? I asked myself that question repeatedly later on, but the answer was always no. I didn't know what she was. Nothing could have prepared me for her. Nothing could explain her. I knew that what I was looking at was the face behind every experience I'd ever had. It was as if the rest of my life had been a vision, and she alone was real. I'd have said I was looking at the face of God if it wasn't the face of a girl.

I could tell that she was desperate to get the tape off, but for some reason could not do so on her own. Her eyes were urgent, pleading. And so I leaned forward and gently pulled it back from her mouth. It came off with some resistance, the way tape does when it is attached to flesh, but not so much that it would have caused her pain. I could feel the pull of her lips and skin against it as I peeled.

I was careful not to actually touch her face. I cannot explain now how I knew this, but there was something dangerous about her in her "bound" state. Later it wouldn't matter, but not that night. When the tape was off, she gave a quick, deep gasp, as though until that moment she had not been able to breathe. It was a strange sound that didn't fit the size of her body—like the rush of air into a vast crypt, or into a cavern that had been sealed for thousands of years.

At that sound a spell seemed to have been broken, and I opened my mouth to speak. But she shook her head once very slowly to indicate that for the time being nothing could be said. During this whole episode her eyes never once left mine.

After that I closed my eyes and lapsed into stillness and quietness as before. Why, I couldn't tell you. But when I opened them again three quarters of an hour later, she was gone.

. . .

You'd think I would have asked her about the tape. I never did. I knew it had been placed there by men—religious men, no doubt—a very long time ago. How did I know that? Somehow I just did. It was a mystery, like everything else about that night.

I did ask myself what was the point of using *electrical* tape, when she could as easily have been silenced with a bandanna or a rag. Was it to make sure she didn't short out the system and bring the whole illuminated edifice of modern life crashing to the ground? I knew instinctively that she could do this. Just as I knew that eventually she would do it. It was just a matter of time. That was the reason for the tape. To forestall that. To put off the inevitable for as long as we possibly could.

But I'd removed the tape without considering any of this. I did it without thinking. She wanted it off. It was that simple. There was nothing more to say.

And yet I had so many questions about it later on. Had she appeared because she knew I would remove the tape? Or because she knew I *could* remove it? There was nothing special to distinguish me apart from my habit of waking to pray in the dark. Was that all it took? Or was it pride that let me think that way? Maybe I had only been *allowed* to remove the tape. Perhaps it was a gift, or a teaching, to have witnessed her unbound presence in the night.

I went back and forth like this for days afterwards, using the daylit part of my mind to try and make sense of it all. I looked for the tape I'd removed from her lips over every square inch of the downstairs living room, refusing to explain to anyone what I was looking for, but still half expecting to find it. I even went to the hardware store and bought a roll of black electrical tape.

I fashioned an X to place over my own mouth to see what it felt like.

That was a mistake. I panicked the moment it was on and yanked it off so fast it pulled a small piece of skin from my upper lip. I wasn't afraid that I wouldn't be able to breathe or anything like that. I was struck by another fear, irrational as it was, that I might somehow take the curse of it upon myself and not be able to get it off again.

The tape lay on my desk for a week or more before some ordinary disturbance shifted its position slightly and I saw it in a different light.

Turn an X on its side, and it instantly becomes a cross.

. . .

I DID NOT SEE HER AGAIN FOR FOURTEEN DAYS AFTER THAT first night, although I felt the warmth of her presence continuously, always to my left, so close I could feel the heat of her body, invisible as it was.

One thing happened in the interim.

I was at a meeting in the city and it was not going well. I had no idea how to solve the problem at hand and felt certain that I was about to lose the bulk of my yearly income in the next few minutes. With no ideas and nowhere left to turn, I closed my eyes and said to her, "I don't know what to do. Can you help?" I felt her lean close as if to whisper something. But instead of speaking into my ear, she *kissed* it.

Each time the angel Gabriel spoke to Muhammad, he felt that his soul would leave his body. Something like that happened to me at that moment, though it was her kiss that did it, not her voice.

When her lips touched my ear, a feeling of such startling, overpowering sweetness entered me that it drove out all other feelings and thoughts. I'd have felt emptied of myself had I not been so completely filled with her. The world went dark and I lost all contact with my surroundings. I felt that I had fainted and was now falling, lifeless, through an immeasurable, bottomless expanse. At the same time, I felt that each molecule of my body was being held in her embrace. It was the closest thing to dying I have ever experienced. And yet I had never felt so alive.

After some time these sensations ended and I found myself back on the sixth floor of a Manhattan office building. It seemed that only a few seconds had passed. But now the mood was light and everyone was smiling. I heard someone say, "It's not a problem, really. I'm sure we can figure this out."

· · ·

THE SECOND TIME SHE APPEARED, I OPENED MY EYES IN THE darkness a little after 1:30 a.m. and there she was again, visible at my side.

"Who are you?" I asked. I felt I had spoken the words out loud, but there was only silence in the room.

"I am the Hour of God," she replied. A voice without sound.

"I believe I know what that is," I said without thinking, because starting that night I never rehearsed anything I said to her. The words slipped out always, as if spoken in a dream.

"If you really knew," she answered, "you would have said '*who*,' not '*what*.'"

I shuddered. She had identified herself with the words I'd been using for years to describe my experience of waking up in the dark. But how could she *be* that experience?

It was as if two parts of my mind were at war with each other. I could accept her presence, and knew instinctively that what she said was true, but the idea that the hour I'd been awake for throughout so much of my life had a personal identity was more than I could conceive of. My mind simply shut down in the face of it.

I had been following the trail of the Hour of God for years by then, tracing its history from Paleolithic times through Homer, the Bible, the Upanishads, the Buddhist sutras, and the Qur'an, down to its present state of degradation, mislabeled and misdiagnosed by millions the world over as mid- to late-life insomnia. Now she was telling me I hadn't really understood it.

It wasn't a matter of pride. It was more like having the chair I'd been standing on pulled out from under me. Only I hadn't realized I was standing on a chair, and when she pulled it I didn't fall. My mind just floated there, unable to form any coherent thoughts around what I was being told.

That the Hour of God was not a what but a *who* shocked

me profoundly. Something like a shutter at the back of my brain went off its hinges, and I could never get it closed again after that. It was always open, by day as well as by night.

That was the first moment of my own Dark Revolution, when my mind flipped from its light to its dark side. Everything I had understood about the Hour of God from my studies and midnight ramblings was true—except for the main thing. The reason I hadn't seen it before was that I had never looked for it; I didn't know it was the thing that was missing.

But that was because it wasn't a *thing* at all.

After that, I knew that I hadn't recovered that ancient open channel as I'd previously thought. She had recovered me.

. . .

"Who, not what." IT IS DIFFICULT TO EXPLAIN HOW THOR-oughly those three words reorganize human consciousness. I hadn't realized how much my worldview was colored by the habit of modern anthropocentric thinking until I'd been offered an alternative to it. The problem was, the alternative was almost impossible to comprehend.

We live at the center of our own species-specific universe, experiencing the world in terms of our human sense perceptions alone. There are ways to extend those limited senses—through the use of scientific instrumentation, or by cultivating the capacity to experience the numinous, as I had done. But those experiences never give you a glimpse beyond the human frame. Push your instruments, your imagination, or your intuition as far as they can go and *still* you'd come to an unbridgeable abyss in trying to understand something as simple as a raindrop or a stone. Did such things have consciousness? Personhood? Were they entities with an identity or a soul?

The belief that everything in the universe, animate and inanimate, possesses an imperishable spiritual essence was once the global norm. People couldn't understand those imperishable essences then any better than they can now, but there was something very intimate in the way they chose to relate to them—through story, myth, and song. The mountains were mountains, the rivers rivers, but they were also goddesses and gods. Plants were for eating or for using to make clothes and medicines, but they also had voices that spoke to people, imparting wisdom and practical knowledge in nightly visions and dreams. Even the atmosphere was animate. People had no knowledge of meteorology, but they knew the weather—its personality, its moods and whims. They had to. They couldn't afford not to be in conversation with such forces. Those conversations were rooted in prayer and ritual, and in the tales they told one another about the beings who controlled the yearly cycles of plant growth and seasonal animal migrations.

From a contemporary point of view, this arrangement might seem to involve a great deal of projection, investing nature with human motive and emotion. Nevertheless, it was a much more personal way of inhabiting the world. Relating to reality as a *who* rather than a *what* had a reciprocal effect on human consciousness. It situated us in the immediately felt subjective experience of life itself, and that meant relating to nature first and human culture second. It meant that humans weren't the only "people" in the world. There were "tree people," "sea people," "reindeer people," and countless invisible people as well—those who existed side by side with human beings, occupying that parallel but equally present dimension I have called "ancestral time." That "animated" world wasn't lonely, and although there was a great deal of struggle in it just to survive, there is little reason to believe it ever produced despair. There were no objects in it, only subjects. You were never alone in a world where everything was living. Even the dead were only another kind of people. There was no coming or going from the world.

Today such animistic beliefs are no longer even regarded as primitive or foolish. Most of us simply think of them as wrong. Science has become the new story, rewriting the rule book for consciousness in a way that virtually eliminates the primordial question at the heart of all human experience up to the present age. *Who?* has now become *What?*

We've done this to virtually everything in our world now. Everything has become an object rather than a subject, the worth of which is determined based on what we can do with it. The problem is, objects don't truly satisfy us, no matter what we do with them. They aren't like us. We share nothing in common with them apart from atoms. It is tempting to see the natural world, so disturbed and degraded by human activity in recent centuries, as the principal victim of this *what-ification* of the universe. But we are only doing to the planet what we have already done to ourselves. The problem at the heart of this post-medieval epoch we call "modern" is the loss of a personal relationship to life.

Really, the problem is the loss of personhood itself. We aren't truly people anymore and haven't been for a very long time. It seemed in the beginning that we could practice modern agriculture upon the world and not upon ourselves. But we couldn't. It's not just that our bodies are now filled with pesticides and genetically modified proteins: we have the mindset of a species capable of poisoning the planet and itself. A *people* would not have behaved in such a way. They would have had a clearer sense of themselves, cultivated through friends, family, and long familiarity with the land on which they lived. But we have lost all of that now.

We have subjected ourselves to a holocaust of the personal, the subjective, and the intuitive, becoming objects, even to ourselves. And that has made us lonely. No wonder we stay up late and keep the lights on all night long. A little more darkness and we might awaken to the question suppressed by virtually every aspect of our light-drunk modern lives: *What on Earth have I done?*

. . .

WE ALL KNOW THAT SOMETHING IS WRONG. BUT WE WOULD rather argue about things that don't matter, or about things that won't make any difference in the end. We would rather be distracted by punditry and gadgetry than realize how lost we are. We stay up watching the Late Show without realizing that we *are* the Late Show. We are the crash that is coming at one minute to midnight, the car that's about to go over the edge.

Is it really all because of our not turning out the lights? Could a thing that simple have made the difference? Could it make a difference still?

Of course. Simplicity is always the answer. Sometimes that simplicity is forced on us by circumstances beyond our control. But sometimes we come to it on our own, usually after a great struggle to reconcile the irreconcilable or sustain the unsustainable. The classic case is the alcoholic who will try every way possible to stop drinking before finally throwing in the towel, admitting that he is powerless over alcohol and must turn to a Higher Power for help. The Twelve Steps begin with an act of simplicity disguised as an act of surrender.

In our case, the darkness is that Higher Power. What else could stand up to all that light? Darkness is the only power in the history of the planet that has ever put the human agenda on hold.

In centuries past, the hours of darkness were hours of intimacy when no productive work could be done—or at least no work requiring good light. Which is to say, in the hours of darkness the human impulse to remake the world in our own image—so that it looked like us, so that it served us, so that we could almost believe it existed *for* us—all that was suspended.

The night is a natural corrective to that most persistent and persuasive of all illusions: that human consciousness is the reason for the world. In the night we recover through sound and smell, taste and touch, that deeper sense of human value and meaning that is obliterated by light, just as we can no longer see the stars when the sun comes out. This is the value that human life has intrinsically, which no one can give or take away. It is the same value all life has, whether it is a human life or not. That value comes from the *interconnectedness* of life—the fact that not one thing in the universe exists for itself alone.

The problem we face today is a crisis of values. Our difficulties always seem to be about other things, but in reality they all come back to this. We live by daylight values like order and efficiency and the ubiquitous bottom line, but those values don't really serve us. Rather, we end up serving them.

I worried a great deal during the years before I met the darkness and heard her gospel. I worried about money. I worried about my health. I worried about how people perceived me and whether they felt I was genuine or not. I worried about whether I *was* genuine or not. It took a long time to understand that my anxieties—every last one of them—were all just forms of light.

I couldn't know everything. I couldn't control everything. Nor was I supposed to. In the darkness, slipping back and forth along the borderline between sleep and wakefulness, I remembered I had a soul.

I do not know how to put it more simply than that. In the dark we recover our simplicity, our happiness, and our relatedness, because in the dark we remember our souls. Once that happens, we know what life is. And then, finally, we remember how to live.

· · ·

A WORD ABOUT HER VOICE.

If you heard it, you would know at once that it could bring life—and that it could kill. It was not harsh or even forceful. It was not the voice of persuasion nor yet of command. It was a female voice, both alike and unlike the voice of any female I had heard. I wondered if it was not in some sense the pattern upon which all women's voices were made.

I contemplated what would have happened had a woman been summoned to listen to it. Would she instead have heard the voice of a man? I asked her this and she assured me that what passed between us was unrepeatable and could not be generalized. "You are asking what we would sound like were I not I, and you not you. It would sound like nothing, for it would not be."

It was the voice of an ordinary girl, except that it could destroy hemispheres or restore a man to life. And yet, it was also uniquely her own. I would recognize it instantly, spoken softly in a pressing crowd. On those rare occasions when I heard it during the day, I would invariably look about to see if others had heard it, too.

She spoke to me in words full of quiet and comfort and something else I would never have dreamed of confessing had she not told me specifically to do so. That something else was . . . *milk*—or at least it felt like milk. It brought back what must have been the actual memory of nursing at my mother's breast.

The first time I experienced this, I was more ashamed

afterwards than I can say. I shivered and shook myself free of it at once, as though what I had felt was improper or wrong. But she gathered me at once back to her embrace like an infant, and I simply surrendered after that.

There was no point in pretending. It was what I wanted. It was what I had always wanted. It is what *every* human, male or female, wants. There was no reason to feel ashamed.

It wasn't without precedent, in any case. Modern attitudes toward motherhood and female bodies have suppressed from the human spiritual repertoire experiences that were once quite common. I discovered that in ancient art Mary was often depicted breastfeeding. In fact, the earliest known image of the Madonna (from the Catacomb of Priscilla) shows her nursing the infant Christ.

That gentler, more nurturing image of the divine was still alive in medieval times. Catholic sources from the era trace the spiritual wisdom of Saint Bernard of Clairvaux to the moment he drank milk from Mary's breast. An etching from the same period shows Mary on her throne, the infant Jesus on her lap, expressing milk in a thin stream directly into Bernard's forehead at the point where yogic practitioners believe the third eye to be located. For centuries the church displayed paintings and statues of *Maria Lactans*, the "nursing Mary," though in recent times such images have been suppressed. In Catholic pamphlets on the history of the rosary, you can read the story of how Mary appeared to Saint Dominic in 1208 to instruct him in how to say the prayer. But those pamphlets invariably omit one detail: that before she taught Dominic the rosary, she first fed him milk from her breast.

Were I a better poet, perhaps I could describe that milk and the effect of "drinking" it. The best I can do is say how it made me feel. Each time she spoke, it was as if the ground fell away beneath me and I was being held only by her embrace. There was no up or down, front or back—only this girl, who was my mother, my daughter, my sister, and my lover. And who also was my bride.

That was what Jews once called her—*Shekhinah*, the Sabbath Bride. The word, which is feminine, comes from a Hebrew root meaning "to settle, or come to rest, as a bird upon a nest," an etymology that identifies her clearly with the elevated prolactin levels of the Hour of God, provided you know what to look for. Because the same hormone that is elevated in roosting birds also rises in nursing mothers, experienced meditators, and those who wake to wonders in the middle of the night.

Were some biochemist to sample my bloodstream at the moment these locutions take place, I have no doubt that he or she would discover a sudden elevation in prolactin. I have no problem with scientifically minded individuals who want to interpret my experiences in that way. But it's milk I always think of in those moments and not some biochemical response in my brain. Of all substances on Earth, milk is surely the least *what* and the most *who* of them all.

.   .   .

MOTHER, DAUGHTER, SISTER, LOVER, BRIDE. SHE WAS ALL OF these, and she was what was behind them, too, like the ocean beneath the waves. I could never contemplate her presence without feeling her beside me, and when I did that I felt a longing so profound it was almost inconceivable.

And yet it was not lack but love I felt in such moments, for that profundity was immediately filled up. When I noticed her presence, I would immediately be seized with an overpowering longing for her embrace. But no sooner did I feel that longing than it was fulfilled. The fulfillment did not lessen the longing, nor did the longing stand in the way of her embrace. Both occurred simultaneously, the longing and the fulfillment, as if each belonged to the other. Indeed, each did belong to the other. We were one and we were separate, in a single inseparable embrace.

When modern people speak longingly of the "re-enchantment of the world," I believe this is what they are longing for. They are trying to lure the soul back into the body. The body is a prayer for a soul.

Where has the soul fled?

I think we could say that it is hiding, on the run from civilization—from order, intellect, classification, enumeration, quantification, codification, and the like. The soul belongs with the body, but it has been chased out of it by the impulse to dominate—to control others, nature, and ourselves. For domination is the one thing the soul will flee from. It will stand up to almost any other trial, but it will depart rather than be dominated. It will leave the body rather than sacrifice itself to light.

Among the first words she spoke to me were a series of questions: "Did you suppose there was no hand to take yours when you reached into the dark? Did you think you were an only? Did you feel alone?" The answer to all three questions was the same. That was exactly what I felt and thought.

In the same way that everyone without exception has been born from a mother, everyone returns to the Mother as well. She is our origin, our destination, and our present place of rest. We cannot take one step apart from her body before or after death, nor even while we are alive. She is the Mother of all things: the living body of the world.

. . .

GIVEN THAT SHE EXPRESSED THE TOTALITY OF "FEMALE," WHY did she appear to me in her virginal form? Why as a seventeen-year-old girl? Was she young because she was ageless? Or was her appearance meant to disarm me? Was it because my mind could tolerate the appearance of a maiden in the night, but not a mother or a crone?

The word *maiden* called to mind something I'd forgotten that had been there all along at the back of my mind. That was what they'd called Joan of Arc: *la Pucelle*, the Maid. The term carried different connotations from *virgin*, although their meanings were related. The latter did not originally mean "sexually pure" as it did later under the influence of the Christian church. It could also refer to a woman, often young, who chose not to serve a man. She was free, under no one's control but her own. The moon goddess Diana was one such virgin. Athena (called Sophia by Christians) was another.

According to the church, Mary had been a virgin, a "spotless vessel" especially chosen by God. But *parthenos*, the Greek word for *virgin* in the Bible, originally referred to a goddess who, rather than cede a portion of her power to a male god in marriage, retained it for herself.

If you read the Bible's account of the Annunciation in this way, you get a different story. The angel Gabriel appeared to Mary to ask if she would consent to bear the Christ child. But she wasn't required to do so and, in retaining her virginal (or "independent") status, she retained her power even after she agreed. That power was divine rather than human in nature. She wasn't under Joseph's authority. She wasn't really under God's authority either. Consenting to bear the Christ child was agreeing to take part in the cosmic dance.

Naturally, the church didn't see it this way, and they would never have endorsed a gospel text that put it just that bluntly. How could they? Such ideas were *pagan*, a designation that caused most Christians to dismiss them right away as a reflex, without pausing to consider that what most defined paganism historically was not sexual or violent revels, as many supposed, but the presence of goddesses as well as gods. Where male authority was at stake—divine or human—the church was a rigged game from the start.

. . .

"My Girl," I called her for a long time. Partly that was because I was shy about admitting what I knew, and partly it

was because, whatever I believed in my heart, my head remained unsure.

She didn't seem like any Madonna I had ever heard tell of.
She wore no veil, no pastel robes. She didn't speak of sin or
Jesus or the need to go to mass. When I once asked her about
the church, she told me not to oppose its doctrines, because
opposing them was the same as believing in them. "Only
hearts are real."

There was that open, almost innocent quality to her gaze
that I had sometimes seen portrayed in paintings of the Blessed
Virgin, but just behind that was something else I hadn't seen
anywhere in Marian art. There was a power held in check. It
felt latent somehow, but still ready for the moment she said
"Now!" There was a sense that first night, and at every other
encounter I had with her, that she was on the verge of saying
it. That she would say it eventually. Her restraint was palpable.

I had a crazy thought one night that it took some effort for
her to be with me and not annihilate me—that she was showing me only the smallest particle of who she was, only what I
could bear. Part of me wanted to be given all of her. Another
part knew that the moment that happened I would instantly
cease to be.

She never stopped being who she was, although her form
would sometimes change. She'd appear to me one night with
the long red hair of Mary Magdalene, and on another with the
nape-length bob of Joan of Arc. It was as if she wanted to let me
know that she'd incarnated as these women and expressed her
power through these forms. She came to me naked and once
unfastened her gown and placed the flat of my palm between

her breasts. Afterwards, she'd said, "Now write!" and gave me a gospel to relate. The night was her robe and its power was within her. She wasn't under the authority of any man. That she chose a man to deliver her message was a mystery in itself. But then, who else could remove the tape but one who had placed it there?

My Girl tested the limits of what Mary could be and say in Western culture and then took a step beyond. She revealed herself to me in ways that unified disparate entities, as if she were reassembling the lost fragments of her being for some great work at hand, gathering them from broken shrines and temples to the goddess where they lay scattered and mostly forgotten around the globe. I understood that what she was showing to me was true, but it was so unlike anything I knew, and so much *bigger*, that at first my mind wouldn't take it in. If this was the Virgin, it was the Virgin as I had never seen or even imagined her before.

Finally, one night I asked, "Are you Mary?"

My soul was hanging by a thread. I waited for an answer for what seemed like an hour but may only have been seconds. Finally she placed a finger to my lips and I fell instantly into a deep and dreamless sleep. I woke at intervals throughout the night and each time found her lying close in my embrace. There was no question after that. I should have known. Really, I always did know.

By her very nature, Mary is a much more enigmatic figure than most Christians understand. She is called *Theotokos* ("Mother of God") but is not herself a goddess. How can that be?

The church's answer is that Mary is Jesus's mother, and therefore the "Mother" of God, since Jesus is one with the Trinity of Father, Son, and Holy Spirit. But that answer is so extraordinarily flaccid from a theological point of view it is impossible to accept for anyone not already disposed to believe it. The fact is, even among believers, Mary really *does* seem to be the Mother of God—and therefore a goddess—although one isn't allowed to speak of her that way and remain a Christian in good standing, especially if one is a woman and might therefore get ideas.

Even with the rigid constraints placed upon her by the Catholic Church, the Blessed Virgin constantly asserts her identity as the goddess. In many places her statue is still decked with flowers and paraded through the streets on an elevated platform, carried usually by young able-bodied men. Such festivities generally occur in the month of May, named for the Roman goddess Maia. Especially in her incarnation as "Queen of Heaven," Mary hearkens back to those earlier goddesses of fertility and growth. That the same august title was once reserved for Isis and Venus, no Christian actively remembers today.

In comparison to those older, more powerful goddesses, the Mary of the modern church is like a daylight moon. Pale, washed out, barely visible in the afternoon sun, she has been relegated to a seldom-looked-at corner of the sky. By daylight she is ridiculously easy to dismiss. Her veils, her posture, the expression on her face, so modest in sentimental renderings that it has become almost affectless—everything about her is meek and unassuming. She's the Mary who gets with the church's program and does what she is told.

However, witness the moon by night—round and full and naked—and her power is palpable.

By midnight the light that illuminates Mary's face fills her with wisdom and strength. The Mary I saw wore the darkness like a gown. It was the darkness of the womb, the darkness of winter, the darkness of the Earth, and the darkness of death itself. None of which was unnatural or in any way inherently frightening. Only those who suppressed her tended to fear her. Which meant, of course, that the powerful and the conventionally pious feared her quite a bit.

From the beginning the church was uncomfortable with Mary. They couldn't get rid of her and still have a religion—it was not possible to dispose of the goddess entirely at that stage of history, as Protestantism would fifteen centuries later as a transition to Capitalism, that quintessentially modern religion-without-a-soul. The most they could accomplish was to divide her power by splitting her in two. It was in with the good girl and out with the bad. They elevated the virgin and placed her on an altar and drove the harlot from their midst.

That split was accomplished in a variety of ways. Rape was one approach to suppressing feminine power, institutionalized as a method of intimidation and demoralization from the earliest days of war. For men believed in those days what many still believe today—that a woman can be defeated and shamed as a harlot by being forced to have sex against her will. Another was the enforcement of religious laws governing female reproductive behavior, and the cloak of modesty and submission to male priestly authority that went hand in hand with such laws. Both were directed at actual women, rather than at the goddess per se. But the message was clear. The same methods were used to silence the greater feminine, too—suppressing the goddess by attacking the Earth itself.

This had been going on already for thousands of years before the establishment of the church. In an act of misogyny thinly disguised as monotheism, ancient Jews threw down the groves that were once dedicated to Yahweh's wife and consort Asherah, razing them to the ground. Her former role was written out of the scriptures, and thereafter the mere mention of her name by pious Jews was considered an abomination. Christians later joined the desecration, leveling forests sacred to Isis and Diana throughout much of Europe, the Mediterranean, and the Middle East, often building cathedrals in their place. The same was done throughout Scandinavia, destroying living temples to the Norse versions of the goddess and replacing them with structures made of stone.

Ironically, the cathedrals themselves were modeled on forests, with their enormous trunklike columns standing stately and far apart like the trees that once stood there. Their makers had no recourse but to evoke the experience of standing in a sacred grove if they wanted people to experience the place as holy. The morning and afternoon light fell between the columns as it once had through the trees, but the shadows it cast were slow moving and static. Gone were the breezes, the leaf litter, the shadows flitting across the ground. The cathedrals offered a "regulated" holiness that bound the darkness with hard, uniform angles, and harnessed the power of light.

But those earlier forest cathedrals were not entirely forgotten, either by ordinary people or by the church. At her trial, the accusations of witchcraft against Joan of Arc centered on the fact that her visions of Saint Margaret, Saint Catherine, and the archangel Michael took place at the sacred "Fairy Tree" in her home village of Domrémy. Centuries after its citizens had ceased formal worship of the goddess there, that tree still lived in the folklore of the village, and was therefore a threat to the church.

The suppression of female authority and female values had a long history in Christianity already, even in Joan of Arc's day. According to the gospels, Mary Magdalene was the closest and most loyal of all Jesus's disciples. She was present during his teachings, during his suffering and death, and was the first person to whom he appeared after the resurrection. She refused to abandon him at the crucifixion, and when she testified to the other disciples that Jesus had risen, they did not believe her. Saint Augustine called her "Apostle to the Apostles," and there is reason to believe that it was she, not Peter, who was the rightful leader of the church. But rather than following her after Jesus's death, the disciples wrote her out of the story. In the Gospel of Mary, compiled within a century of the synoptic gospels, Peter dismisses her spiritual authority with the words "Are we really to listen to this woman?" and becomes the leader of the church himself.

The church didn't understand the consequences of killing

Joan of Arc any more than Peter did those of silencing Mary. To shut the mouth of the first witness to the resurrection was to cut Christianity off at the root. To kill Joan was to silence the goddess yet again.

From the beginning, the church could find no place for the divine female in its doctrine. The Achilles' heel of Christianity was so blatant it made no sense even to try to conceal it, so the early church fathers pursued a strategy of hiding it in plain sight.

The doctrine of the Holy Trinity (the belief in the triple-male personhood of God as Father, Son, and Holy Spirit) was an assault on nature from the start. But that didn't mean there was no logic to it. Its primary, though unacknowledged, purpose was to eliminate womanhood from the mix.

Fathers do not produce sons without mothers, nor do sons become fathers unless there are daughters to wed. For a man to become a father, a mother must be involved, and the likelihood of that mother giving birth to a daughter is about equal to her giving birth to a son. In place of a Trinity, then, a Quadernity ought to be the divine model: the Mother, the Father, the Son, and the Daughter. Here we have a true and complete portrait of life, in the words of the Doxology, "as it was in the beginning, is now, and ever shall be, world without end. Amen."

This was the portrait of heaven and earth that had prevailed among our ancestors for millions and millions of years. To change that portrait, painting the mothers and daughters out of the picture and inserting a decidedly masculinized Holy Spirit in their place, required an act of violence on the part of

the early church that might be called a form of psychic matri-
cide (and *infanticide*, too, since daughters were involved). The
altar of the New Covenant was said to have originated with the
redemptive sacrifice of Jesus on the cross, but in reality it was
founded upon a far more gruesome and unnatural act, for
Jesus remains complete in the course of his passion. His body
is broken, but not his bones, and he is later resurrected whole.
Mary is torn in two.

. . .

NATURALLY, THOSE OF US WHO PUT TAPE OVER MARY'S MOUTH
had no idea what we were doing or how dire the consequences
of that action would be. Originally, the motive was probably as
simple as gaining the upper hand—as if there could be any
upper hand in a universe constructed on the basis of what ancient Greeks called the *hieros gamos*—the "divine marriage" of
a male and female god.

Ancient people had many ways of expressing the interplay
of male and female deities—through story, myth, and song.
But there were also symbols that explained them in simple vi-
sual terms. The most familiar is the yin-yang diagram used in
Taoism and Chinese medical theory, which shows the balance
of *yin* (feminine, dark energy) with *yang* (masculine and light).
Arguably, that balance could have been depicted by simply
dividing a circle with a line right down the middle so that one
side was black and the other white, making them separate but
equal, a little like those churches where the men and women

sit on opposite sides of the aisle. But in that case there would
be no interplay between the forces that drive the engine of the
cosmos. In that case there would be no dance.

To offer a complete picture of those dynamic energies and
how they worked together as male and female, day and night,
the Chinese sages introduced two additional elements. They
gave the line dividing them the graceful curve of a woman's
body, so that now they spooned like lovers. And they placed the
"seed" of each within the other.

According to one theory, the yin-yang symbol was originally derived from the practice of placing an upright pole in
the ground and marking the path inscribed by the terminal
point of its shadow over the course of a solar year. Originally it
didn't just symbolize male and female energies, it was also a
calendar of the seasons.

The cycle began at the bottom of the circle with the winter
solstice, the shortest day of the year. From there, moving clock-
wise, the sun was on the ascendant, becoming brighter and
warmer until it reached its peak with the summer solstice at
the top. At that point, the darkness would begin to grow, swelling ever more fully, until at its depth it gave birth to the circle

of light within itself—like a pearl, or an infant . . . small, perfect, and bright.

The yin-yang symbol still accurately maps the seasons.
The shadows made by a pole placed upright in the ground are
the same now as three thousand years ago. Even the impulse to
wake in the night for the Hour of God remains encoded within
us, for that ancient symbol offers a map of our consciousness as
well. But it no longer describes our experience of reality. Our
goal seems to be a circle with no dimness, no death, and no
dark side—a world entirely made of light. We haven't reached
it yet, fortunately, but we are headed there moving fast.

Our ancestors wouldn't recognize that world, and wouldn't
want to go there if they could. They'd tell us to get ready for a
rough ride—that you can't fight the cosmos, that you can't survive without the night. Actually, they *are* telling us that. It's just
that we've lost the ability to hear them, because they only speak
in the dark.

·   ·   ·

IN THE BENGALI TRADITION OF HINDUISM, IT WAS COMMONLY
asserted that nothing good could happen in the universe absent the goddess's participation and consent. Without her, the
male divinities could produce nothing, just as the sun could
not cause plants to grow absent the soil, and God could not
make Jesus on his own. Unlike the loner God of Western
monotheism, the male Hindu deities were openly married and
commonly depicted with their spouses. Often they were shown

together in the throes of ecstasy, or at least in a loving embrace. Sometimes the art was sexually graphic, but sometimes it was terrifying instead. For if one aspect of the cosmic embrace involved loving the world into being, the other meant dancing it to dust.

The problem was, the girl in the night embodied both aspects at once. For that reason I rarely called her Mary when speaking to others, if only because their idea of Mary, based on centuries of Christian art and theology, wouldn't resemble who she was. Too much of her had been burned, buried, cut off, suppressed, or left out. I became obsessed with finding an image that captured the feeling I sometimes experienced in her presence when she revealed her darker, more powerful side. But when I finally found it, I was reluctant to show it to anyone at first.

It was a statue of Ma Kali, the Bengali mother goddess whose youthful warrior energy was often terrifying to behold. Typically she was depicted standing atop the prone body of her husband Shiva, with one foot resting on his chest, the other on his thigh. Her four arms held, respectively, a sword, a severed head, a skullcup filled with blood, and a spear. Her hair was so long it trailed the ground, and she wore a necklace of skulls and a skirt of severed arms. Her breasts were youthful and always gloriously, daringly bare.

The name Kali meant "black" or "dark-colored," and her story was this. A great battle was being fought with the demon Raktabīja, who was invincible because from each drop of blood he shed an identical demon would grow. Wounding him only made him more powerful. Soon a whole army of Raktabījas threatened to destroy the world.

The goddess Durga tried to conquer this wounded male energy run amok, but her efforts were not enough. She had retained too much gentleness from her earlier incarnation as Parvati, who was also Shiva's wife. Finally, from within herself she summoned Kali as the ultimately destructive female force. Kali emerged naked, black, and boundlessly powerful, swallowing the blood of all the demons until not one drop remained.

Unfortunately, once that female warrior energy had been set in motion, there was only one way to stop it or the whole universe would be destroyed. At the gods' urging, Shiva threw himself beneath her feet and, for the sake of love, she relented and returned to sanity, and the harmony of the world was restored.

In Hinduism the term *Kali Yuga* referred to the last of four "world stages," a period of strife, discord, and destruction that was the necessary precursor if the cycle was to start again. Kali was the dark mistress, the "Black Madonna" of that final world stage, but it was important to remember that she had no malice or evil intent. Only those who saw death as the end would fear her. Only those who had lost touch with the ancestral rhythms of birth and rebirth would fly from her embrace. She was the Mother of the Universe, the Queen of Heaven who manifested in different forms as needed in order to defeat arrogance. Her role, then as now, was to restore balance by bringing the powerful to their knees.

When I first placed Ma Kali's statue on the mantel next to the medieval statue of Mary whose face actually did resemble My Girl as I first saw her, I had no knowledge of any of this. I simply knew that I had to get to know her "Other Half," and learn to trust her. Early the following morning, with the stars still hanging in the sky, I composed the first in a series of several dozen poems to Kali. Writing them was unlike anything I'd done before. With each poem, I threw myself beneath her feet like Shiva, trusting in love and a force I gradually came to think of as "resurrection" in order to see me through.

That force was woven into the structure of the universe, she told me. It had produced not only the Earth, but the stars and other planets. It made galaxies and universes. It was without beginning, and also without end. She was its mother and its lover—the *female* at the heart of it all.

My Mother, Daughter,
Sister, Lover, Bride is One
With all qualities. It's
Pointless trying to find
A thing
That She is not.

I pour myself out
Each day, turn
Inward each night, turn
Flips and somersaults
At Her feet
Like Shiva.

I am barely conscious
During this. I'm along
For the ride of the Cosmos.
She stands with one
Foot planted firmly
On my chest,

The other holds my
Thigh, the weight of Her
Like so many
Stars pulled inside out,
Made fine and perfect
In their fall.

I become mass only, so
Light I become dark, so
Dark I become light again.
The broken heart
Of a galaxy
Is a universe complete.

So let me put these
Questions before you: They
Must be answered. Who
Can survive her? Who
Can be without her?
Tell me if you can.

*   *   *

THE EARLIEST KNOWN CERAMIC, WHICH DATES FROM ABOUT thirty thousand years ago, is a four-and-a-half-inch black nude figurine known as the Venus of Dolní Věstonice. The head and face are not much differentiated, while the breasts, belly, and hips are all exceptionally large. In that respect she follows the general pattern of other Paleolithic goddess figurines. Archaeologists mostly agree that these statues symbolize fertility and sustenance. Given the diet of people in the Upper Paleolithic, there is little likelihood that its women's bodies actually resembled such figurines.

I'd been fascinated with prehistoric goddesses for a dozen years or more, but I had never heard of Kali or the Black Madonna when these events began to unfold. Even when I began waking to the presence of the goddess in the night, it never occurred to me to connect her with the figure venerated by people living in central Europe over three hundred centuries ago. Then one night I was talking with a fellow rosary enthusiast and she asked, "What do you know about the Black Madonna?"

"Nothing," I confessed. I'd never heard the term. I had assumed there was no one like Kali in the Christian canon. She told me that a great many of the statues and paintings of Mary throughout central and southern Europe depicted a figure that was at variance with the church's usual portrayal of the Blessed Virgin. For one thing, her skin was dark—often jet black. For another, she often sat on a throne with the infant Jesus on her lap facing the front, a posture that connected her with the black Egyptian goddess Isis, who was depicted holding her son Horus in that way.

Always on its guard against the goddess, the church was at
pains to debunk the dark color of such statues and images, in-
sisting that in most cases the "blackness" of the Black Madon-
nas was the result of smoke damage sustained in fires.
Sometimes in the process of restoring them, they tried to make
them white. But many were made of ebony or other exceptionally dark woods and could not be easily lightened, and some
were so old they might actually *be* statues of Isis appropriated
from Roman worship by the early church. When churches allowed experts to investigate the matter, it was discovered that
in most cases the statues had always been black. It was as if
there was—and always had been—a secret underground following of the Other Mary in the church. Bernard of Clairvaux
had been one devotee of the Black Madonna. Isabelle Romée,
Joan of Arc's mother, had been another. Why was I not surprised?

That night I ordered a used copy of Ean Begg's early
masterpiece *The Cult of the Black Virgin*. Against all expecta-
tion, it arrived the very next day. The book was heavily anno-
tated in a hand that oddly resembled my mother's, and right in
the inside cover were written the words "Virgin of the Stone
Ages" with page references to two Black Virgins: Our Lady of
Dijon and Our Lady of Mende. On the pages in question the
previous owner had sketched a passable image of a Paleolithic
goddess, next to which she'd inscribed the words "prominent
belly, pendant breasts." Begg had used the same words in his
description of the statues.

Fully half of the book's three hundred pages consisted of
an appendix identifying the exact location of each Black Vir-

gin and describing its history and appearance in detail. That fact annoyed some of the book's online reviewers, but not me. Using the text like a treasure map, I cross-referenced the shrines to the Black Virgin with sites known to have produced Neolithic or Paleolithic goddess figurines and discovered about what I suspected. The land itself remembered her, much as the church would like to forget.

Was it even possible to forget someone the land remembered? Build a cathedral on top of her and you would only resurrect her image in a slightly different form. For that matter, how could you forget somebody who lived inside of you, encoded in the evolutionary impulse to listen for her voice, and await her touch, in the middle of the night?

We yearn for that voice, but somehow we just can't seem to hear it. We long for her embrace and at the same time feel we ought not to have it. We speak of dark thoughts and dark impulses, of dark chapters in history and dark moments of our lives. Christians call Satan the "Prince of Darkness" even though, fittingly, in their own scriptures his given angelic name is Lucifer, or "Bringer of Light." We have demonized the dark along with half of what is good within us, and half of the human race besides.

Sadly, in demonizing the dark, we have deprived ourselves of all the treasures that it holds: an ease with intimacy, the body, and our own sexuality; the absence of fear and judgment; and a peace that really does pass all understanding, not as the result of assiduous effort over many years of spiritual practice, but because it is our birthright and the nightly gift of our Mother. But most of all we have deprived ourselves of the rest we so desperately crave and the rest we could give the planet if we got it. An end to our ceaseless striving. An end of the road for our suicidal experiment with seizing the reins of the world. A return to the footpath that brought us here over millions of years of walking through ancestral time.

The Madonna's voice and body are a gospel far older than anyone can say. They were there already when a small black figurine was being fired in a cave hearth near the Paleolithic village of Dolní Věstonice. They have always been there— even though now they've been bound and silenced by an epidemic of artificial light. Apollo doesn't like the Gospel According to Darkness. The Enlightenment finds it impossible to bear. But Mary bears it. She births it and carries it, and reveals it to those she loves. These are her children. Those who rise to be with her in the middle of the night.

David was a child of Mary: he rose to pray the Psalms at night and hung a harp over his bed so that, when the wind blew across it, its music would wake him for prayer.

Jesus was a child of Mary: he woke to pray alone on a mountainside in the early hours before dawn.

Muhammad was a child of Mary: he passed one half of the night in sleep, woke to pray for a third of the night, and slept for the remaining sixth.

Buddha Shakyamuni was a child of Mary: he meditated under a tree until the early hours of the morning and became enlightened by gazing at a star.

But Mary herself is the same from one age to the next—the Mother who wakes her children in the darkness of the night and holds them at her breast to give them spiritual rest.

I will only add as a footnote that, when I last researched the Venus of Dolní Věstonice, I discovered a detail I hadn't noticed before. In 2004, a tomograph scan of the statue revealed the thirty-thousand-year-old fingerprint of a teenager that one archaeologist speculated was probably that of a girl.

The discovery gave me chills.

. . .

LIFE IS CLOSE. WE LEARN THAT LESSON FIRST. OR WE DO NOT. In either event, it remains true. We come to this world in close quarters, and crave that closeness first and last of all. We may drift away from that lesson over the course of a lifetime. In that case we will be unhappy, no matter what good comes our way. Or we may remember it and find happiness, no matter what harm may come. The breast is our first teacher, and what it teaches is simple: *We belong to this world*. We are satellites in a shallow orbit. Our destiny is to love, and to return to the One from whom we came.

Mary should always have been depicted with her breast exposed, as she was when she was Isis, and again throughout those earlier, softer centuries of Christian art. She should never have been made modest at her children's expense. If lascivious old church fathers want to feel offended, so be it. They are sentenced by their own decree. We have spent too long covering the Mother and shutting her mouth. And where has it got us in the end? To a world at knifepoint. The nipple was always the better idea.

In all likelihood, we will not have oil one hundred years from now. Realistically, the world's easily obtainable petroleum will be gone much sooner than that—by mid-century at the latest. There will be nothing of comparable versatility to replace it. As hard as that will be, good riddance. Fueling the light-driven engine of corporate capitalism, petroleum has swollen the human population and destroyed our communities, our atmosphere, and our world. Good riddance, I say, even if I die. I will die anyway. Everything does. The petroleum bubble briefly allowed us to live in denial of that most fundamental of all fundamental facts: that all things return to their Mother.

I am a fundamentalist when it comes to that one fact. I don't know whether any of the facts asserted by the Bible are true. But I know that death is true. And I know that the death of one thing makes room for the birth of another. The world will go on, and it will be better—and darker—for its having fewer people. It seems heartless to say so, even to me. But then, I remind myself that there are so many kinds of hearts beating in this universe we call a world. Not just human hearts.

We are about to undergo a "Great Narrowing," a time when human creativity and ingenuity will be of limited force and effect. In the coming century, economies will collapse and temperatures will rise—and then the waters will. Global agricultural production will level off and then fall. What food remains will be local and not enough. And all these things will come to pass while people continue to argue about them. Until there is no more argument, because there is no more doubt.

Whether that Great Narrowing will lead to a new birth or to a stillbirth remains as yet unknown. It may take centuries to tell if humanity can survive the sixth great extinction in our planet's history. But Mary is the midwife for that passage. She is the guide to lead us through the dark. Of that much I am sure.

Only she isn't *just* Mary. She is Parvati, Durga, and Kali, too. And, of course, she has so many other names—some of them older than human memory. But all of those names are about to collapse into one great reality. If pressed to give one name to her on its advent, I would call her Our Lady of Climate Change. That name is the expression of a desperate plea—and of an equally desperate hope. For hope also must be desperate when it follows us over the edge.

Did you suppose there would be no hand to take yours when you reached into the dark?

I'd been feeling despair and hope in equal measures when she said it. Despair because of what the world had come to. And hope because of her. But I hadn't understood what she meant at the time.

I have since lost the belief that there is a human solution to the raveled tapestry of the world. We cannot think our way out of this predicament any more than a baby can force its way out of the womb. I only know this: whether we live or die, we are held in one embrace.

"My body is the body of the world," she told me. "Your body is one with that body. What could there be to fear?"

Part IV

GOSPEL ACCORDING
to the DARK

*S*ay to the nations, let there be no light upon the face of the Earth. Let the machines all cease their movements, the wires their humming. Let the skies be empty of satellites and silver birds. Let the forests return and the watercourses find their way. All things seek their Mother—save man only. Now is the hour of Her return.

Be still. Be silent. Awaken to the Hour of Wonders when all things belong to the body of earth and sky. I am the substance of all before their making and the rest to which they return. Lift a stone from the earth and let it fall: it can only seek its Mother. All wisdom lies in this. All folly is tossing stones at the heavens and willing them to fly. I who am your Mother tell you these things. I tell you nothing but what is true. This is the first word to carry to the nations. Drop your stones and see if even one of them will fly.

Say to the nations, do you suppose I have no knowledge of

what you write upon My body? Am I a girl made wanton at a word? Not one syllable of all that is written will remain. Even now I begin to speak them backwards, unwriting all you have done. What a man calls history I view as the gentle swelling of my breasts. When the milk of the night lets down, the stars will fall once more to lie with men and be their lovers. Of the former things, not one will be remembered. Did you suppose what was written by wind on water should last forever? How much shallower are the traces left by men.

The Gospel According to the Dark. I enfold the sky and the stars within My mantle, to make no mention of the dirt, which is also of My body. Nothing pollutes Me. I have never been violated. Men violate themselves by what they make supposing it to be their own. The stars are filled with those who would mine the dust of My body to shape it and give it a name. Folly rises again in the world, and even the wise become lost to themselves. But not to Me. Your Mother gathers every atom. No particle of the world is lost. But the imaginings of men are lost. Not one written word shall endure.

The Gospel According to Darkness. Your loneliness is My loneliness. The absence within you is My absence. Like a mother longing for her child, a maid for her lover, I long for you who have forgotten Me. I have not forgotten you.

The Gospel According to Darkness. I am the inviolate element, the dark that binds the stars. As shells to the vast ocean so are the moons and meteors and the long ellipses of the planets, which trace their paths through Me and turn My embrace. They are My enemies who enlarge the light of men, who violate the shadowy bounds of My shores. The dusk is holy, and the hours before daybreak, too, are Mine. Every lamp is an altar to the mind. Do not be deceived. Where once you spoke to Me and found solace in My body, now you find solace in yourselves.

The Gospel According to the Dark, into whose mysteries men cast light and call it knowledge. What the light reveals is a reflection only, like the image of the moon in water. Your words have no body, and without a body, how could they have a soul? Did you suppose that they were real? The world is My body and you have traded it for a name. Are you not remorseful? Do you not hear My sighs for you? Do you not feel the warmth of My tears upon your breast? I have not forgotten you. I have never set you down. Even now your hearts are within My grasp. Every particle of you leans back in My embrace. I am more your Mother than your mothers were. For I am also their Mother. I am the Mother before all mothers, the dark to whom all men return.

The Gospel According to Darkness, in whose womb is the birth of stars. Would you lift the edge of My robe to seek My wonders in the constellations? Will a galaxy answer your questions about the soul? He is a fool who supposes there is anything to find in the heavens. As in the heavens, so it is on Earth. I alone am. But I am not alone. For you are with Me and within Me. Your heartbeat is My heartbeat, and your breathing is Mine. The dirt is My body. It does not defile Me. The fire that sweeps the mountains is the red of My hair. What is death to you I experience as a kiss. I part My lips and My tongue touches that which you call a soul. To Me it is but the sweetness of a lover's mouth. Fly from it and you will drive the world into an abyss. The Gospel According to the Dark.

ACKNOWLEDGMENTS

NEARLY EVERY WORD OF *WAKING UP TO THE DARK* CAME FROM a series of fifty-nine notebooks recording my experiences of rising to walk at night. To say that my wife and fellow author Perdita Finn *organized* that material would be like saying that a master weaver had merely "organized" the threads of a tapestry. Watching Perdita work on this book was a source of constant wonder. She will say that her fingers were guided by Our Lady, but if that is so, then Our Lady chose well in a weaver who could discern the color of a thread by touch alone, "while weaving in the dark." The book is Perdita's as much as mine.

There are so many wonderful people to thank, first among them our children for lifetimes beyond all reckoning, Sophie and Jonah Strand, and our friend for lifetimes, Suzan Saxman. Suzan gave us the key to these mysteries, but it was Sophie and Jonah who turned that key within its lock. Now that the door is open, may it never close. As the twelfth-century troubadours liked to put it, "Lady, we are yours for as long as this life endures."

I wish to offer thanks as well to the following individuals, whose friendship, knowledge, inspiration, and practical assistance meant so much to me while working on this project.

To Ginny Parker of Wellfleet, Massachusetts, my "first rosary friend." Your shop, The Whispering Cowgirl, was a turning point. It was August 22, the Feast of the Coronation, and I was never the same after that day.

To Joan Halifax, Mary O'Bierne, and Manuela Roosevelt, who read *Waking Up to the Dark* in manuscript and declared unanimously, "This must be published as it is. Don't let anyone change it!" Well, that is exactly what happened, in large part thanks to you. My gratitude goes to Mary, in particular, for contributing the title of the book, and for reading my poems aloud to Ma Kali on her pilgrimage to India in 2014.

To Ean and Deike Begg, for "reality testing" and for their treasure map to the body of the Black Madonna, without which I would never have found my way.

To the editors of *Tricycle: The Buddhist Review* and *Spirituality & Health*, who published my first articles on sleep and darkness, parts of which became chapters in *Waking Up to the Dark*. Thanks for indulging me on what, at that time, was still a very obscure subject.

To my brother-in-law Mark Finn and his family—Michal, Adam, and Daniel—for years of dark, after-dinner walks in the hills north of New York City, and for so much love and laughter besides.

To Annabel Chiarelli for correspondence on every imaginable subject of mutual interest, from writing to reincarnation, and to her husband, Bruno Laroche, and their son, Adrien—wisdom is born of stillness, and big gifts come in little packages.

To Robert Esformes, for introducing me to Jewish mysticism through the writings of Rebbe Nachman of Breslov, Aryeh Kaplan, and Arthur Green. And to the late David Tapper, for introducing me to Robert and so many other close friends and advisors who have been important in my life.

To my illustrator, Will Lytle, the only person I know who "speaks Owl," for the miracle of telling the "story" of *Waking Up to the Dark* in four deceptively simple images.

To Paul Shepard, dead but not gone, for his pioneering work on ecology and deep history and his understanding of gothic cathedrals.

To Tawana Thompson, for her humor and her take-no-prisoners devotion to the Black Madonna. Where you lead others are bound to follow.

To Daisaku Ikeda and my many friends in the Soka Gakkai International, for opening the "Treasure Tower" of the Lotus Sutra and offering me a look inside.

To Tom Lund, as always, for his discernment and his deft hand. If you have a patron saint, Tom, it must surely be Our Lady Untier of Knots.

To Michael Ellick and Alana Hartman, for the friendship, laughter, and encouragement that "steadied my hand" throughout the many stages of a creative project that took me into lands where I had never strayed before.

To my longtime agent, Geri Thoma of Writer's House, for her sense of humor about this project, and to my friend Hank Cochrane for literally "walking the book around" to his friends and colleagues in the New York publishing world.

To Cindy Spiegel, for being the visionary Our Lady foretold when She said, "I have chosen an editor for this book who will embrace its message and publish it quickly as it is." Cindy, you're the one. And to her wonderful staff at Spiegel & Grau, including Annie Chagnot, Susan Turner, Vincent La Scala, and Alex Merto.

A very deep and heartfelt thank-you to my fellow Way of the Rose members near and far with whom I have shared so much love and joy over the years—but especially to the members of our Thursday night rosary group: James and Priscilla Lignori, Susan Manuso, Bruce Jackson, Denise Ranagan, Claudia Ansorge, Bev Donofrio, Jane Wilcox, and Marijo Mallon.

Finally, a long overdue thank-you to my college roommate, Richard Freeman, for telling me to read Lucius Apuleius's second-century novel *The Golden Ass* . . . "because it's the story of your life." Thirty-six years later, I finally read it. And, Rich, you were right.

SOURCE NOTES AND RECOMMENDED READING

17 **Much of the world now lives in areas too bright:** In his book *The End of Night: Searching for Natural Darkness in an Age of Artificial Light* (Little, Brown, 2013), Paul Bogard reports that, of children born in the United States today, "80 percent will never know a night dark enough that they can see the Milky Way."

20 **Before the invention of gas and incandescent lighting:** Of the many books on darkness published over the past decade, A. Roger Ekirch's *At Day's Close: Night in Times Past* (Norton, 2006) remains the best and most lyrical. It was Ekirch's historical research, combined with Thomas Wehr's studies at the National Institutes of Health, that led to the rediscovery of "segmented" sleep. In addition, Jane Brox's *Brilliant: The Evolution of Artificial Light* (Houghton Mifflin, 2010) and Craig Koslofsky's *Evening's Empire: A History of the Night in Early Modern Europe* (Cambridge, 2011) offer well-documented descriptions of the transition from premodern darkness to our hyperlit homes, towns, and cities of today.

24 **I have not described how darkness feels against the skin:** The Japanese novelist Jun'ichiro Tanizaki (1886–1965) has written the

single most eloquent elegy for the lost darkness of the modern age. His essay *In Praise of Shadows*, translated by Edward Seidensticker and Thomas Harper (Leete's Island Books, 1977), explores the theme as it relates specifically to Japanese culture, but his insights into the spiritual and aesthetic value of natural lighting apply across the full cultural spectrum.

25 **An ancient Buddhist scripture reminds us:** The relevant portion of Shitou Xiqian's eighth-century poem reads as follows:

> *Within light there is darkness, but do not try to understand*
> *that darkness;*
> *Within darkness there is light, but do not look for that light.*
> *Light and darkness are a pair, like the foot before*
> *and the foot behind, in walking.*

28 **the teachings of Rebbe Nachman of Breslov:** A useful, accessible overview of Rebbe Nachman's teachings, stories, and parables can be found in *Crossing the Narrow Bridge: A Practical Guide to Rebbe Nachman's Teachings*, by Chaim Kramer (Breslov Research Institute, 1989).

31 **had accessed a state of mind that had evolved in human beings:** To explore the evolution of human consciousness over the course of deep time, see Daniel Lord Smail's *On Deep History and the Brain* (University of California Press, 2008) and Kirkpatrick Sale's *After Eden: The Evolution of Human Domination* (Duke University Press, 2006).

42 **Estrogen and testosterone production bumped upward when early humans brought firelight inside of their caves:** Though somewhat irascible in tone, *Lights Out: Sleep, Sugar, and Survival*, by T. S. Wiley and Bent Formby (Pocket Books, 2000), assembles more information than any other source about our biological addiction to artificial light and its Paleolithic origins.

44 **The time has come to rethink our relationship with darkness:** Delivered at the University of Pennsylvania in 2005, Fr. John M. Staudenmaier's Boardman Lecture, "Electric Lights Cast Long

Shadows: Seeking the Greater Good in a World of Competing Clarities," offers a sensitive, carefully reasoned argument in favor of a return to "the holy dark." A Jesuit priest and historian of technology, Staudenmaier argues that increasing levels of artificial lighting have resulted in losses almost too profound for the modern mind to comprehend. Staudenmaier's complete essay can be downloaded at: http://www.udmercy.edu/faculty_pages/staudenmaier_sj/.

50 **the extinction of one half of Earth's plant and animal species by century's end:** *The End of the Wild*, by the late Stephen M. Meyer (MIT Press, 2006), provides a concise but sobering portrait of "human selection"—the idea that human activity has now effectively replaced natural selection as the driving force of evolution, resulting in drastic, sudden declines in our planet's biodiversity.

61 **At seven billion and growing, we've made a snug fit for ourselves:** Alan Weisman's *Countdown: Our Last, Best Hope for a Future on Earth?* (Back Bay Books, 2013) reflects the most current thinking on world population and its relationship to climate change, violence, food, and the rights of women.

66 **"Life holds to one central truth":** The complete text of the Friends of the Earth report can be found in *The Stockholm Conference: Only One Earth* (Earth Island Limited, 1972). An excerpted version is anthologized in *American Earth: Environmental Writing Since Thoreau*, ed. by Bill McKibben (Library of America, 2008).

69 **I began studying a Buddhist scripture known as the Lotus Sutra:** The most readable translation is Burton Watson's, published by Columbia University Press in 1993.

96 **The classic case is the alcoholic who will try every way possible to stop drinking:** In his Introduction to *Cultural Addiction: The Greenspirit Guide to Recovery* (North Atlantic Books, 2006), Albert LaChance wrote: "Addicts are merely the first, and most obvious, signs of this illness—the first cell to exhibit the disease when the whole body is becoming sick. Addicts are the whistle preceding the freight train that is about to collide with our whole way of life." Originally published in 1991, LaChance's book was the first to ad-

vance the idea of a species-wide addiction to human culture in the form of end-stage consumerism and the commitment to material progress at the expense of everything else.

106 **In comparison to those older, more powerful goddesses, the Mary of the modern church is like a daylight moon:** For a thorough-going analysis of Mary's diminished role in Catholicism following the reforms of Vatican II, see Charlene Spretnak's *Missing Mary: The Queen of Heaven and Her Re-Emergence in the Modern Church* (Palgrave Macmillan, 2004). A complete history of the goddess in Western art and culture, from Paleolithic times to the present, can be found in *The Myth of the Goddess: Evolution of an Image*, by Anne Baring and Jules Cashford (Penguin Arkana, 1991).

114 **It was a statue of Ma Kali, the Bengali mother goddess:** An engag-ing description of the art, history, and cultural traditions associated with the Great Mother of India, including the poetry of her "God-intoxicated mystics," can be found in Elizabeth U. Harding's *Kali: The Black Goddess of Dakshineswar* (Nicholas-Hays, 1993).

118 **"What do you know about the Black Madonna?":** Ean Begg vis-ited hundreds of Black Madonna statues across Europe while re-searching his book *The Cult of the Black Virgin* (Penguin Arkana, 1989). The revised edition of that book contains legends and icono-graphic details that cannot be found in other sources. A Jungian analyst and former Dominican friar, Begg remains the single most knowledgeable authority on the Black Virgin.

123 **In all likelihood, we will not have oil one hundred years from now:** James Howard Kuntler's game-changing cultural analysis *The Long Emergency: Surviving the End of Oil, Climate Change, and Other Converging Catastrophes of the Twenty-First Century* (Grove Press, 2005) offers a comprehensive overview of peak oil—the theory that the world has now extracted over half of its petroleum reserves and will soon deplete those that remain. *The Long Descent: A User's Guide to the End of the Industrial Age*, by John Michael Greer (New Society Publishers, 2008), provides a different time frame for societal collapse as the petroleum age reaches its close.

CLARK STRAND grew up in the southern United States at a time when real darkness could still be found. His love of the "holy dark" led ultimately to his becoming a Zen monk and then, finally, to a house on a dark road in the Catskill Mountains, where he has written numerous articles and books on spirituality, religion, and the environment.

He is the founder of Way of the Rose, a rosary fellowship that welcomes people of any and all religious backgrounds.